Circle the Number

Name: ____________________ **Date:**__________

Circle the number that matches the amount of objects.

7 8 9 6	4 5 7 6	3 1 2 6
5 4 3 6	1 8 7 5	1 2 3 4
4 3 7 5	0 1 3 2	[illegible] [illegible] [illegible] 5

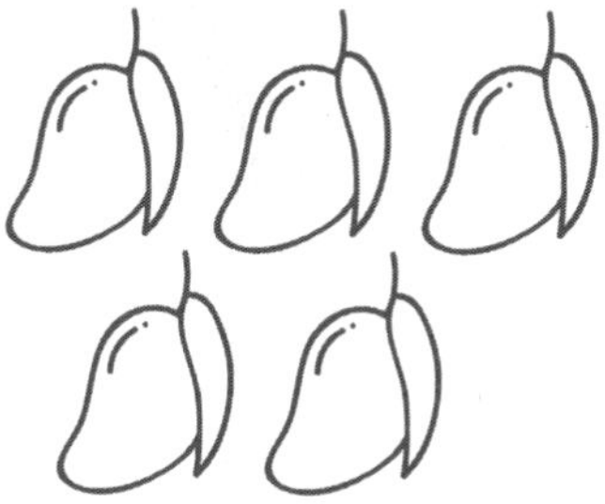

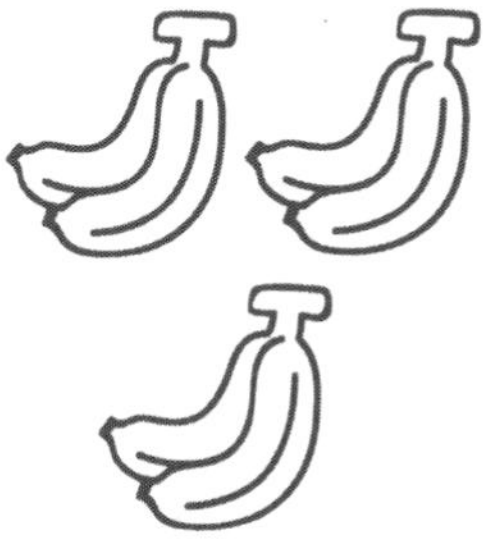

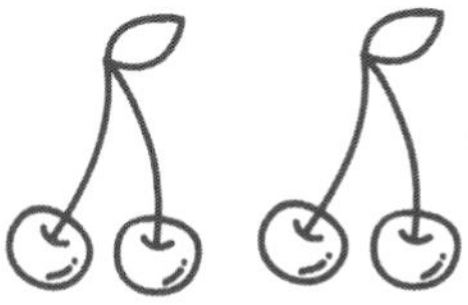

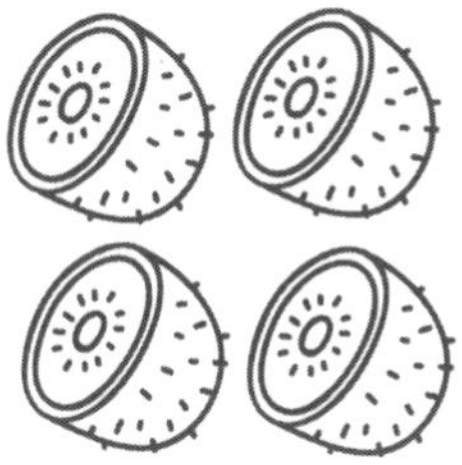

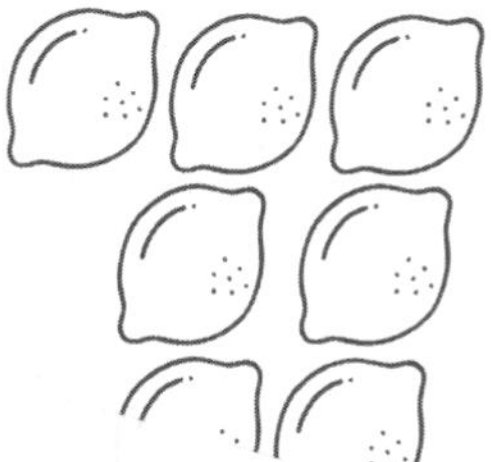

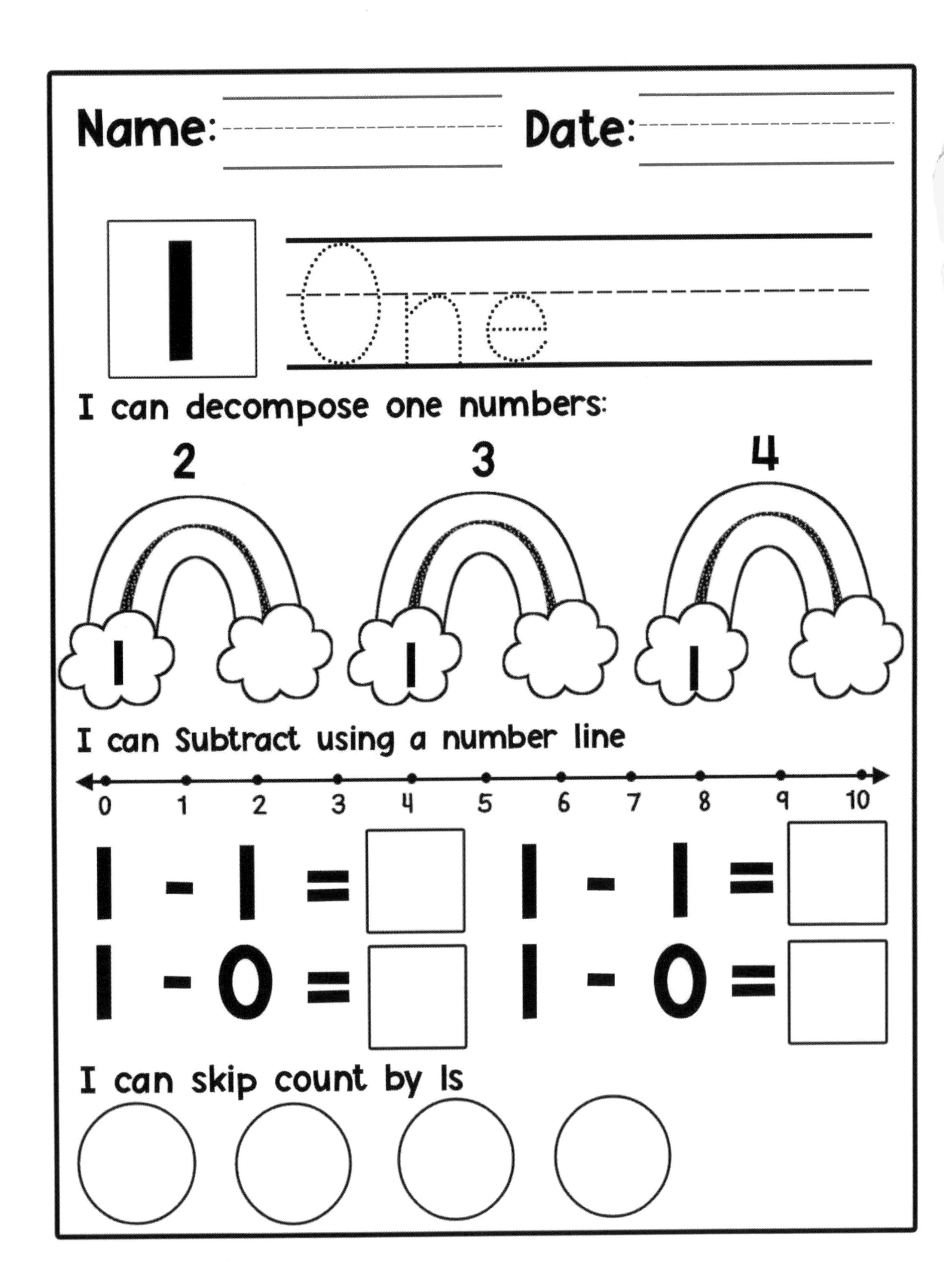
Name:
Date:
1
One
I can decompose one numbers:
2
3
4
1
1
1
I can Subtract using a number line
0
1
2
3
4
5
6
7
8
9
10
1 - 1 =
1 - 1 =
1 - 0 =
1 - 0 =
I can skip count by 1s

Name: ______________ Date: ______________

I Know My Numbers 1

Trace it

One One One One

Write the missing number

0 ☐ 2

Color the number word

One

Color 1 cloud

Draw 1 dot in the bus

Find the number 1

1	3	2	6
1	4	5	7
6	8	6	5
8	9	7	4
2	9	0	3

Show the number using ten frames

Circle the Number

Name: ______________________ Date:___________

Circle the number that matches the amount of objects.

 5 4 3 6	 7 3 4 5	 3 1 2 4
 5 4 3 6	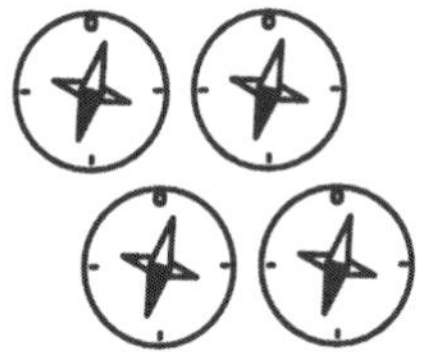 1 8 7 5	 8 7 5 4
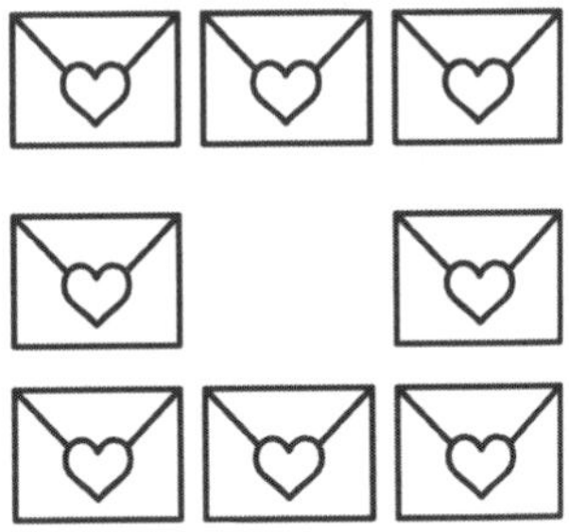 9 8 6 5	 4 1 3 2	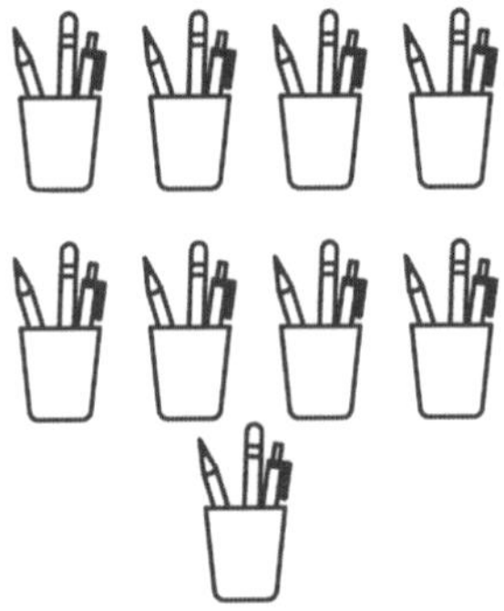 7 9 8 6

Name:

Date:

•Color it

1

•Find the numbers 1

1	8	5	2	8
3	1	6	10	1
2	3	1	5	5

•Trace and write it

1

One

•Follow the numbers 1 through the maze

Start		9	10	7	8	6	5
1	1	1	2	3	4	4	5
2	3	1	1	1	1	Finish	

Name:

Date:

Read It!

One

Write It!

Color It!

One

Color It!

How many syllables?

4	3	6

Trace It!

One

Find It!

Zero	Two
One	Three

Write the missing number!

0 ☐ 2

Color 1 star!

☆☆☆☆☆
☆☆☆☆☆

Name:

Date:

I can read it!

One

I can write it!

One One One One

I can color it!

One

Find it!

One	Five
Two	Four

Circle it!

1	2	3	8
3	1	6	9
4	5	5	7

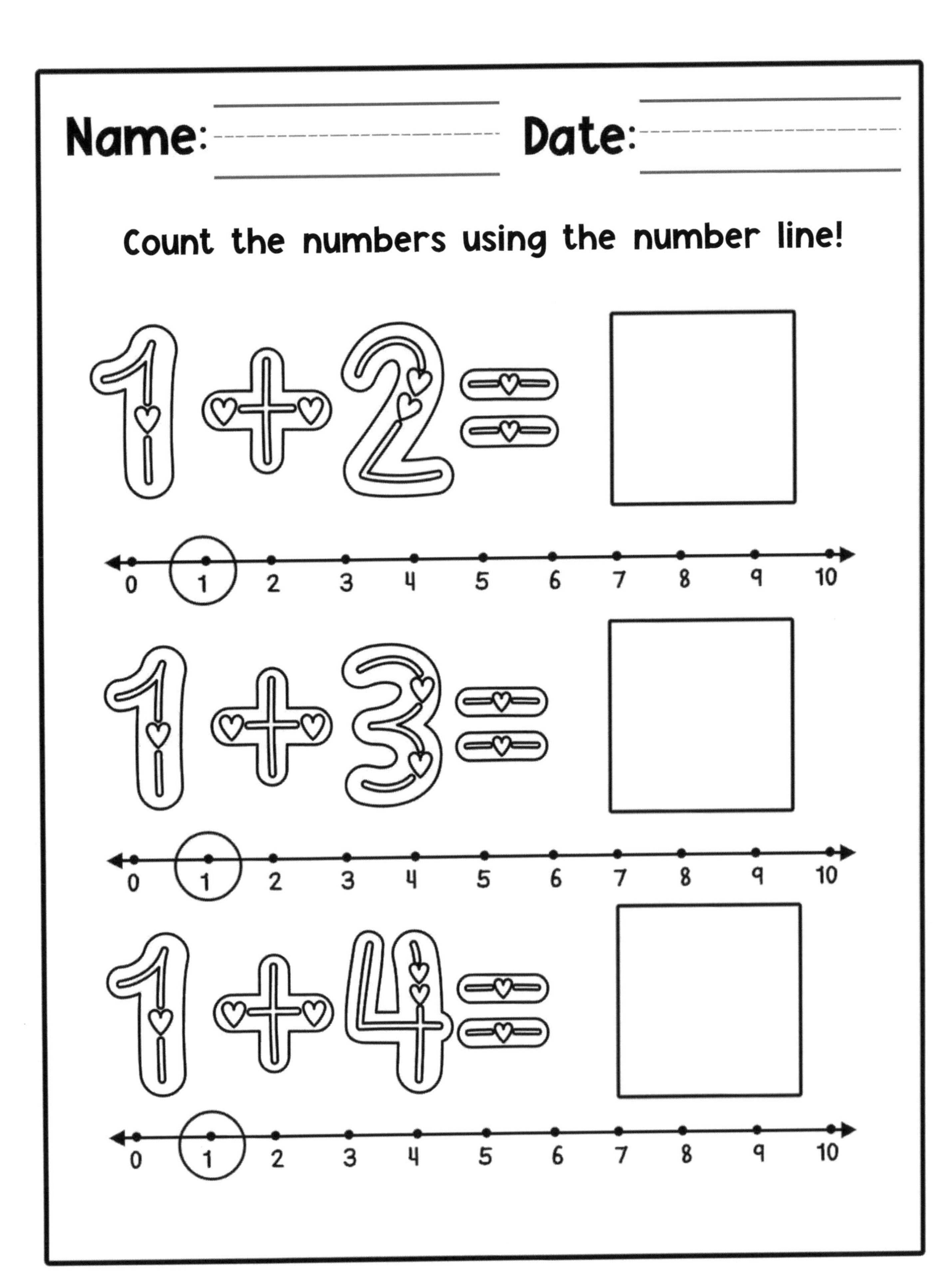

Name:
Date:
Count the numbers using the number line!
1 + 2 =
0 1 2 3 4 5 6 7 8 9 10
1 + 3 =
0 1 2 3 4 5 6 7 8 9 10
1 + 4 =
0 1 2 3 4 5 6 7 8 9 10

Name: ______________ Date: ______________

1.Dab the Number 1

1 2 1 2 3

2.Color 1 star

3.Trace the number

1 1 1 1 1 1 1 1 1 1 1 1

4. Trace the number word

One One One

Name:

Date:

Color 1 apple

Trace the number 1

Trace it

One One One

Circle the Number

Name: ______________________ **Date:**___________

Circle the number that matches the amount of objects.

 5 4 3 6	 7 9 8 6	 3 1 2 4
 5 4 3 6	 1 8 7 5	 8 3 5 4
 1 3 2 5	 4 1 3 2	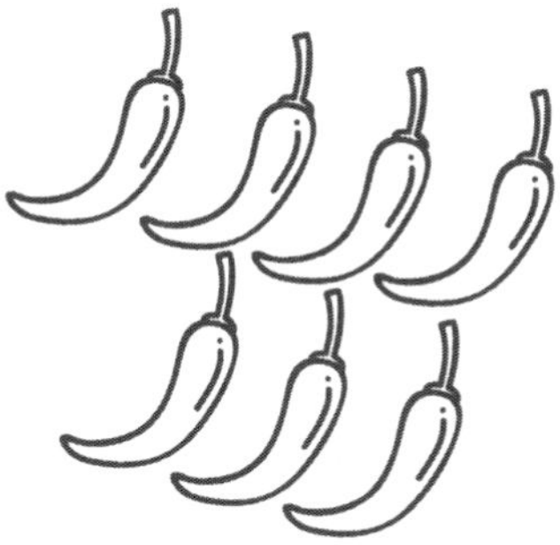 7 6 3 5

Name: Date:

2 Two

I can decompose two numbers:

2 3 4

2 2 2

I can Subtract using a number line

0 1 2 3 4 5 6 7 8 9 10

2 - 1 = ☐ 2 - 1 = ☐

2 - 2 = ☐ 2 - 0 = ☐

I can skip count by 2s

Name: ______________ Date: ______________

I Know My Numbers 2

Trace it

Two Two Two Two

2 2 2 2 2 2 2 2 2

Write the missing number

0 1 ☐

Color the number word

TWO

Color 2 cloud

Draw 2 dot in the bus

Show the number using ten frames

Find the number 2

1	3	2	6
1	4	5	7
6	8	6	5
8	9	7	4
2	9	0	3

Circle the Number

Name: ____________________ **Date:**__________

Circle the number that matches the amount of objects.

 5 4 3 6	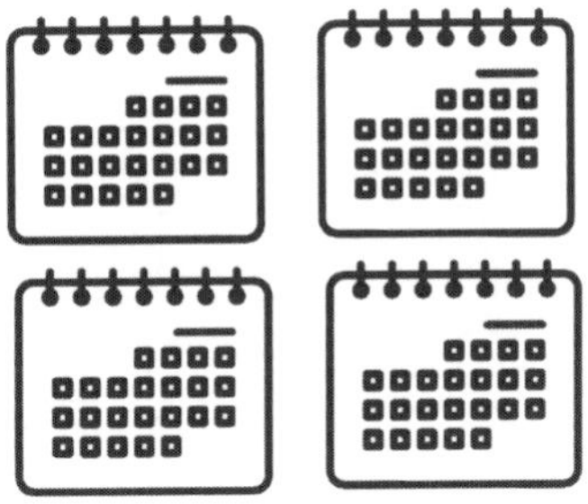 7 4 2 1	 5 1 2 4
 5 4 3 6	 1 8 7 5	 8 3 5 4
 1 9 2 5	 4 1 3 2	 3 4 1 2

Name:

Date:

·Color it

2

·Find the numbers 2

1	2	5	2	8
3	1	6	10	1
2	3	1	5	5

·Trace and write it

2

Two

·Follow the numbers 2 through the maze

Start		2	10	7	8	6	5
1	1	2	2	2	4	4	5
8	3	1	1	2	2	Finish	

Name: Date:

Read It!

Two

Write It!

Color It!

Two

Color It!

How many syllables?

3 2 6

Trace It!

Two

Find It!

Zero	Two
One	Three

Write the missing number!

0 1 □

Color 2 star!

Name: ______________ Date: ______________

I can read it!

Two

I can write it!

Two Two Two Two

I can color it!

Two

Find it!

One	Two
Two	Four

Circle it!

1	2	3	8
3	1	6	9
4	5	2	7

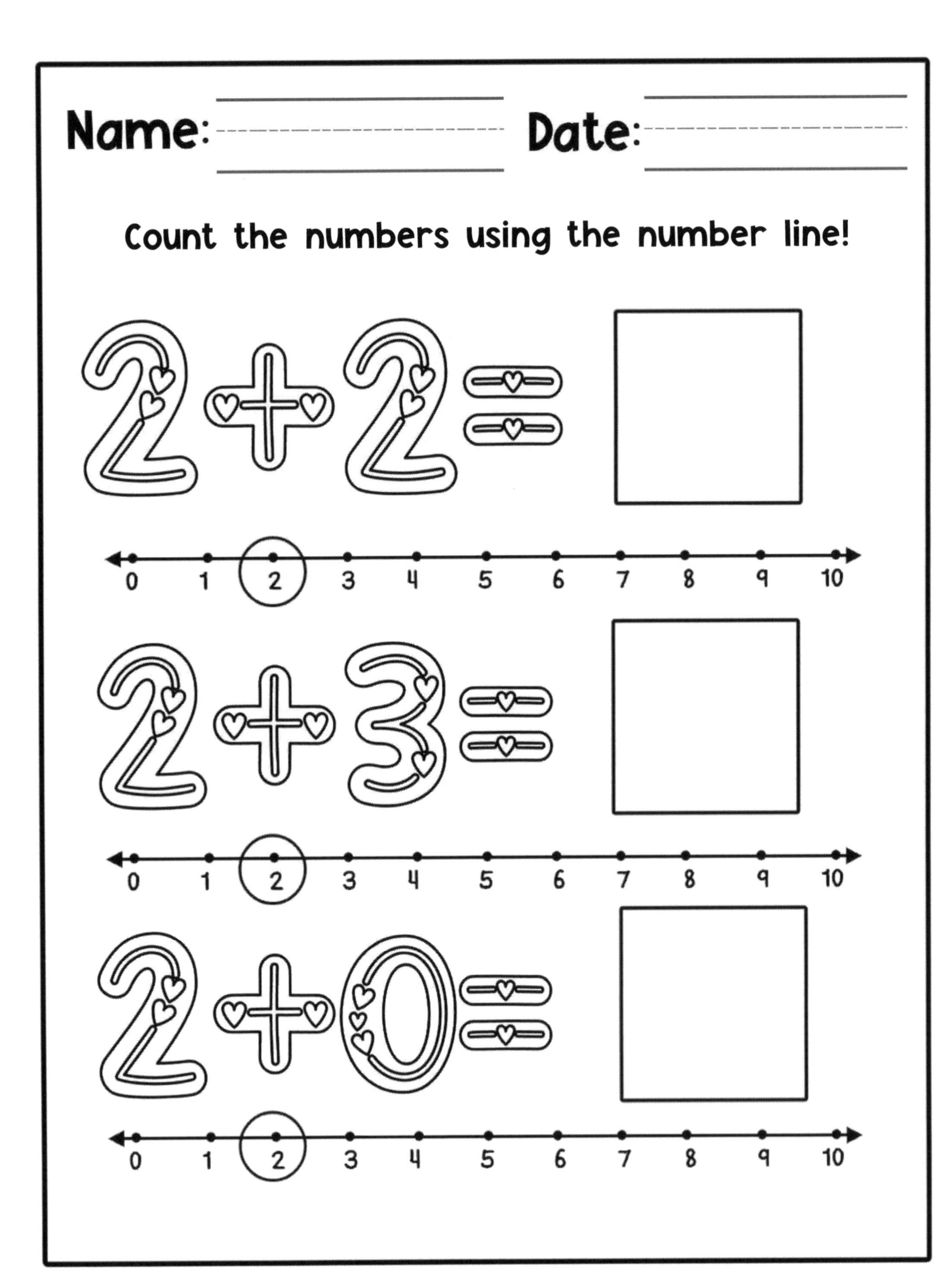
Name:
Date:
Count the numbers using the number line!
2+2=
0 1 2 3 4 5 6 7 8 9 10
2+3=
0 1 2 3 4 5 6 7 8 9 10
2+0=
0 1 2 3 4 5 6 7 8 9 10

Name: ______________ Date: ______________

1.Dab the Number 2

1 2 1 2 3

2.Color 2 star

3.Trace the number

2 2 2 2 2 2 2 2

4. Trace the number word

Two Two Two

Name:

Date:

Color 2 apple

Trace the number 2

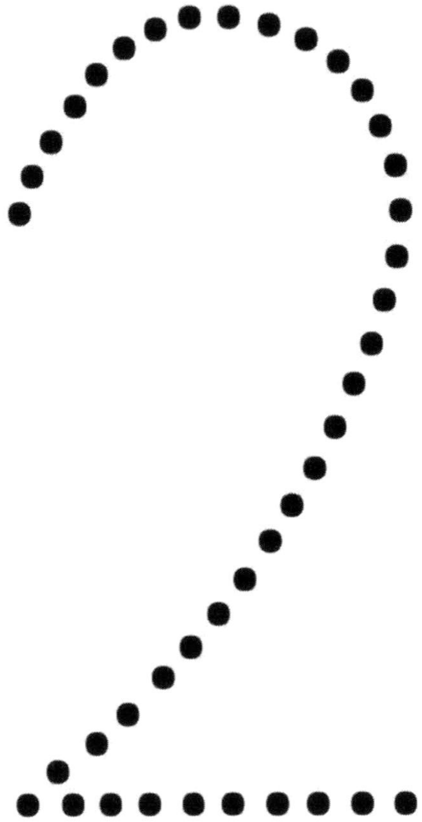

2

Trace it

2 2 2 2 2 2 2

Two Two Two

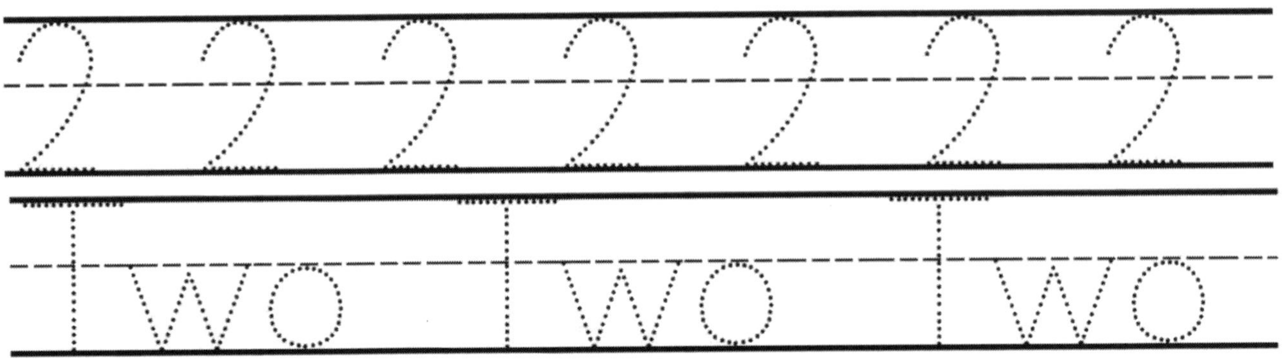

Circle the Number

Name: ____________________ **Date:**__________

Circle the number that matches the amount of objects.

5 4 3 6	7 4 2 1	5 1 2 4
5 4 3 6	1 8 7 5	8 3 5 4
1 9 2 5	4 1 3 2	3 4 1 2

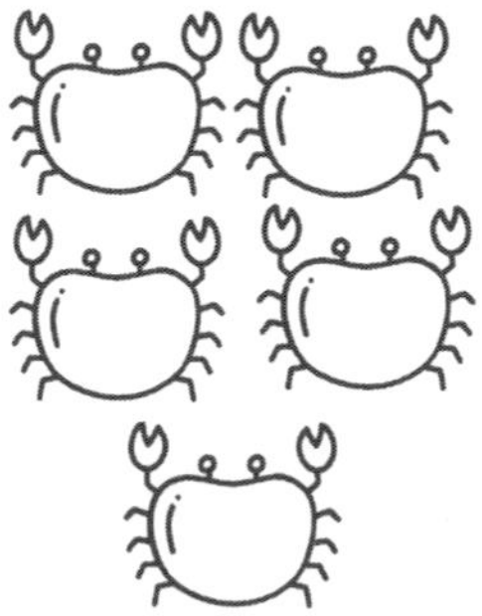

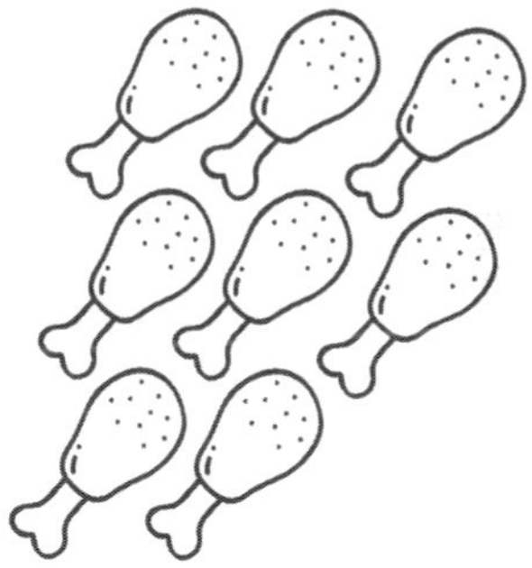

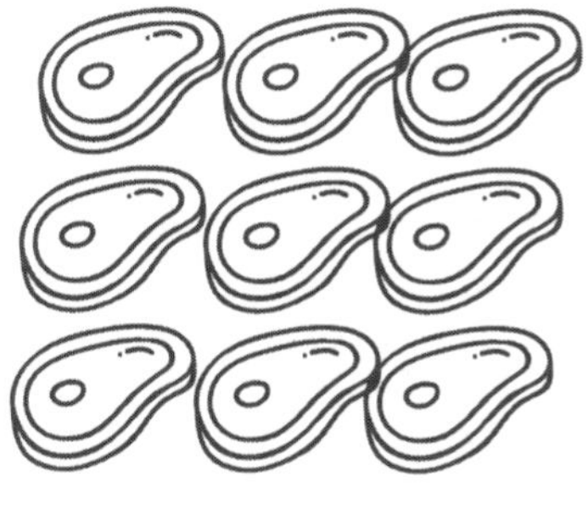

Name: ______ Date: ______

3 Three

I can decompose one numbers:

4 | 3 | 5
3 | 3 | 3

I can Subtract using a number line

0 1 2 3 4 5 6 7 8 9 10

3 - 0 = ☐ 3 - 3 = ☐

3 - 2 = ☐ 3 - 2 = ☐

I can skip count by 3s

Name: ____________ Date: ____________

I Know My Numbers 3

Trace it

Three Three Three

3 3 3 3 3 3 3 3 3

Write the missing number

☐ 4 5

Color the number word

Three

Color 3 cloud

Draw 3 dot in the bus

Show the number using ten frames

Find the number 3

1 3 2 6
1 4 5 7
6 8 6 5
8 9 7 4
2 9 0 3

Circle the Number

Name: ____________________ Date:__________

Circle the number that matches the amount of objects.

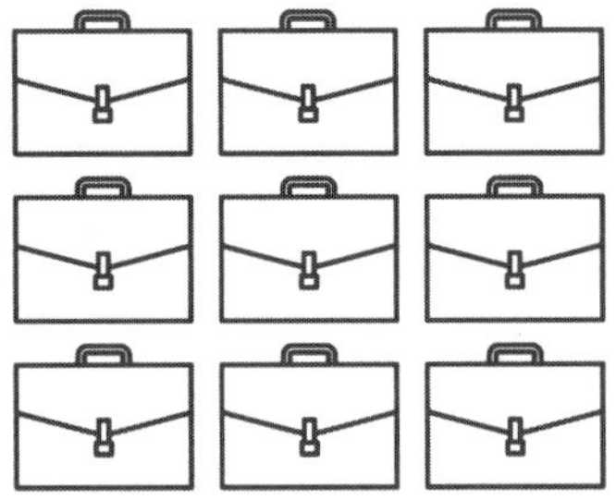 7 8 9 6	 4 5 7 6	 3 1 2 6
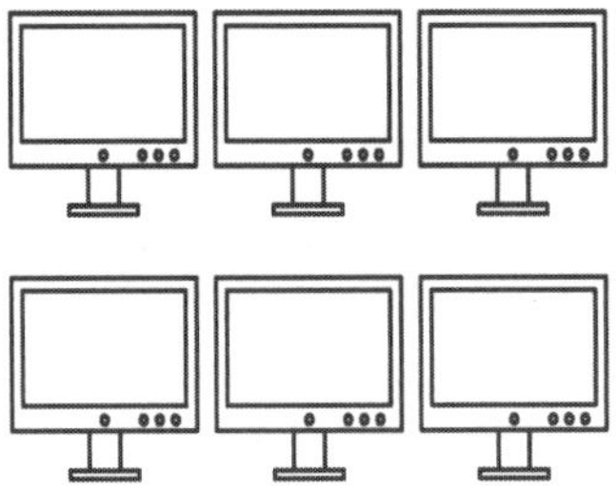 5 4 3 6	 1 8 7 5	 1 2 3 4
 4 3 7 5	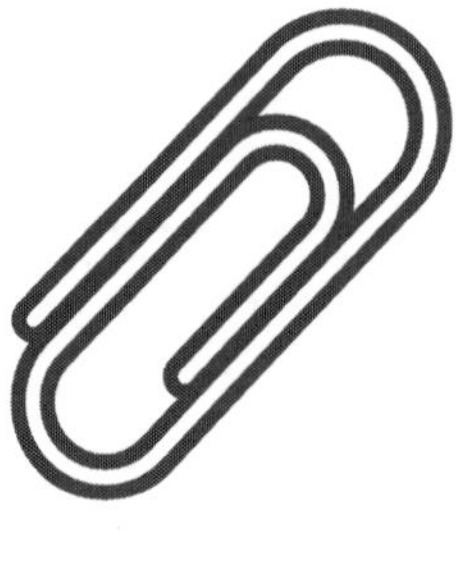 0 1 3 2	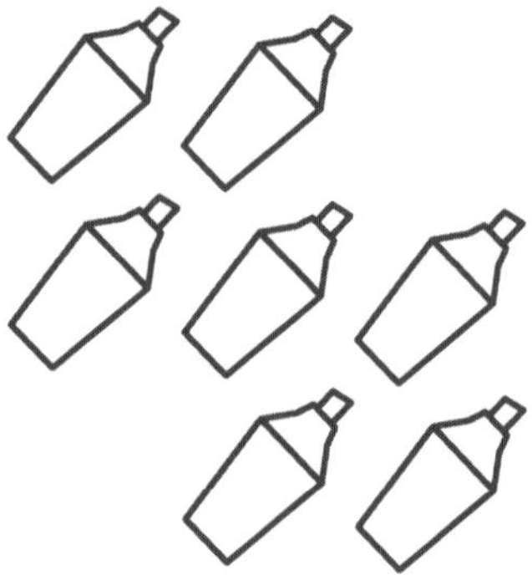 7 6 3 5

Name: ______________ Date: ______________

•Color it

3

•Find the numbers 3

1	2	5	2	8
3	1	3	10	1
2	3	1	5	5

•Trace and write it

3

Three

•Follow the numbers 3 through the maze

Start		2	10	7	8	6	5
3	1	2	2	2	4	4	5
3	3	3	3	3	3	Finish	

Name:

Date:

Read It!

Three

Write It!

Color It!

Three

Color It!

How many syllables?

3	2	5

Trace It!

Three

Find It!

Zero	Two
One	Three

Write the missing number!

☐ 4 5

Color 3 star!

☆☆☆☆☆
☆☆☆☆☆

Name: ____________ Date: ____________

I can read it!

Three

I can write it!

Three Three Three

I can color it!

Three

Find it!

One	Two
Two	Three

Circle it!

1	2	3	3
3	1	6	9
4	5	2	7

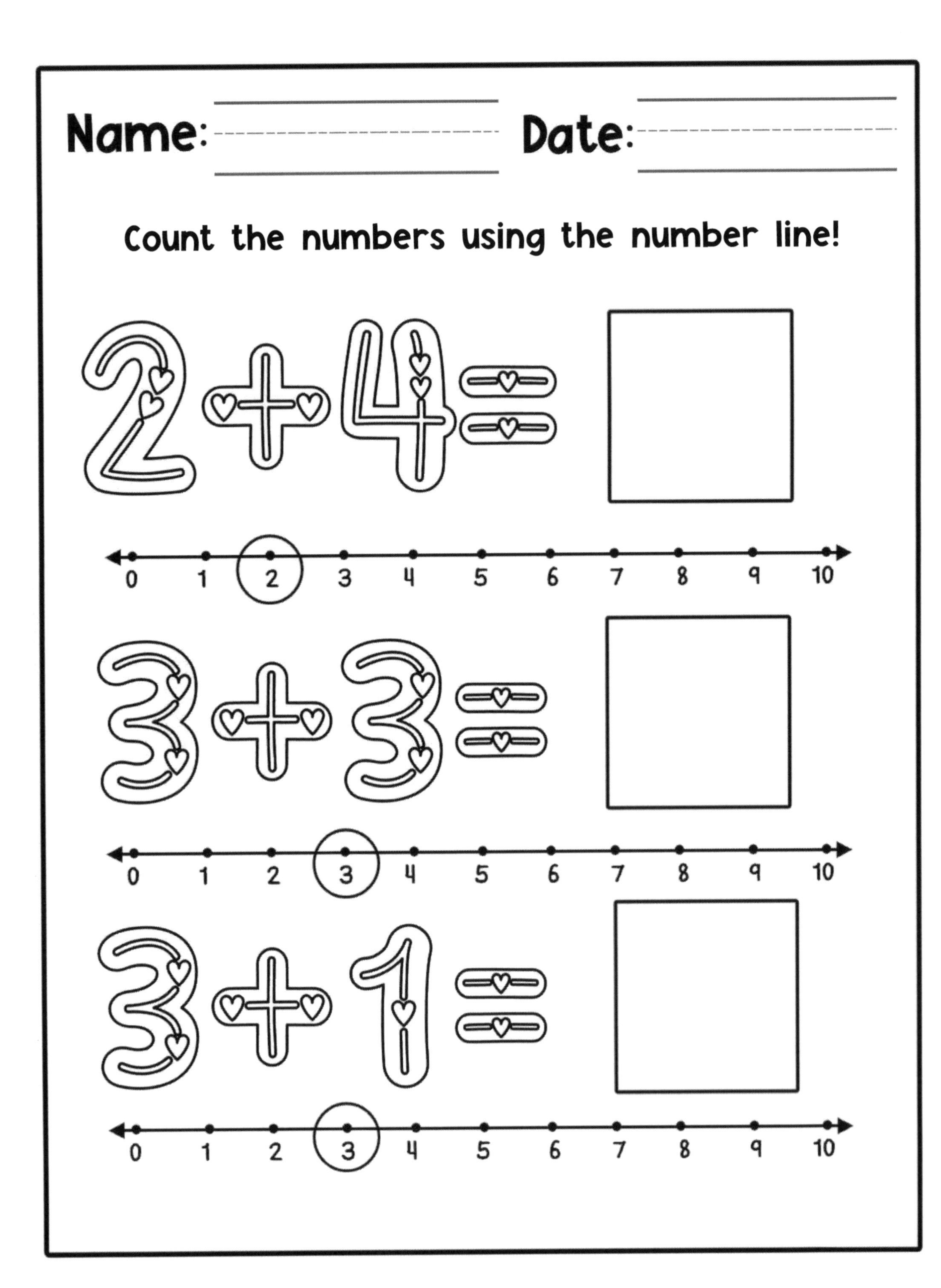
Name:
Date:
Count the numbers using the number line!
2+4=
0 1 2 3 4 5 6 7 8 9 10
3+3=
0 1 2 3 4 5 6 7 8 9 10
3+1=
0 1 2 3 4 5 6 7 8 9 10

Name: ____________ Date: ____________

Count the numbers using the number line!

3 + 4 = ☐

0 1 2 (3) 4 5 6 7 8 9 10

3 + 2 = ☐

0 1 2 (3) 4 5 6 7 8 9 10

3 + 3 = ☐

0 1 2 (3) 4 5 6 7 8 9 10

Name: ____________ Date: ____________

1.Dab the Number 3

1 3 1 2 3

2.Color 3 star

3.Trace the number

3 3 3 3 3 3 3 3

4. Trace the number word

Three Three

Name:

Date:

Color 3 apples

Trace the number 3

3

Trace it

3 3 3 3 3 3 3

Three Three

Circle the Number

Name: ____________________ Date:__________

Circle the number that matches the amount of objects.

 3 1 2 4	 4 3 1 2	 3 1 2 4
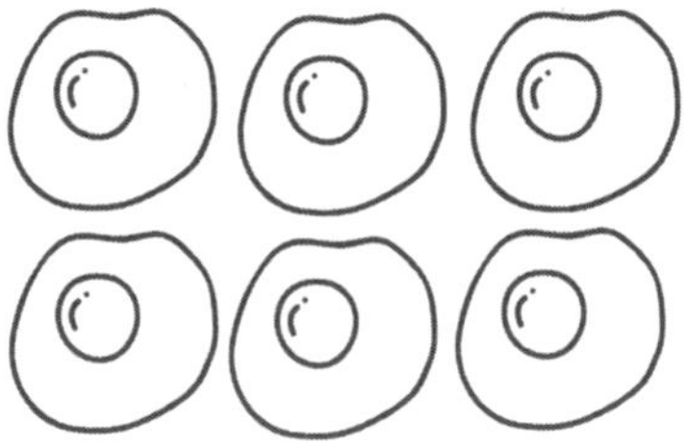 5 4 3 6	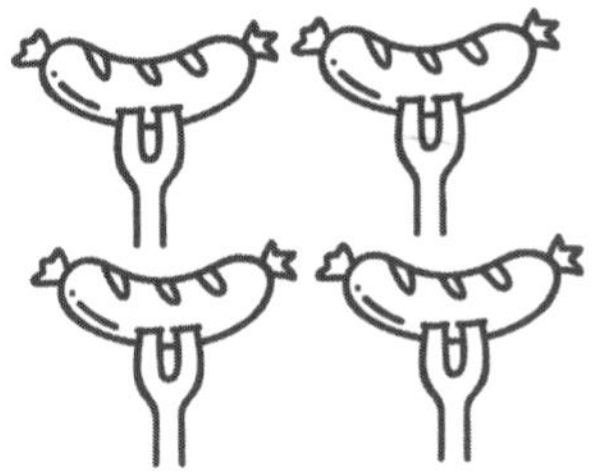 1 4 3 5	 8 3 5 4
 1 8 6 5	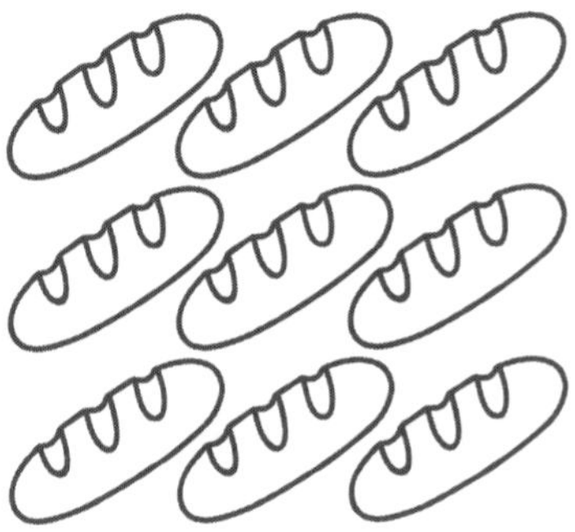 9 1 5 2	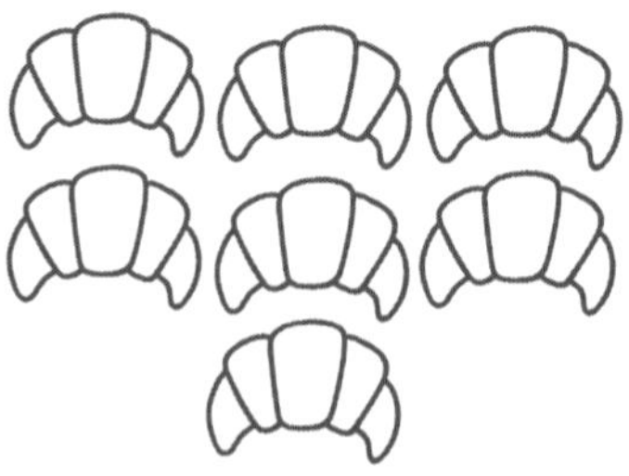 7 6 3 5

Name:

Date:

4

Four

I can decompose one numbers:

4 6 5

4 4 4

I can Subtract using a number line

0 1 2 3 4 5 6 7 8 9 10

4 - 1 =

4 - 1 =

4 - 2 =

4 - 2 =

I can skip count by 4s

Name: ____________ Date: ____________

I Know My Numbers 4

Trace it

Four Four Four Four

4 4 4 4 4 4 4 4 4

Write the missing number

3 ☐ 5

Color the number word

Four

Color 4 cloud

Draw 4 dot in the bus

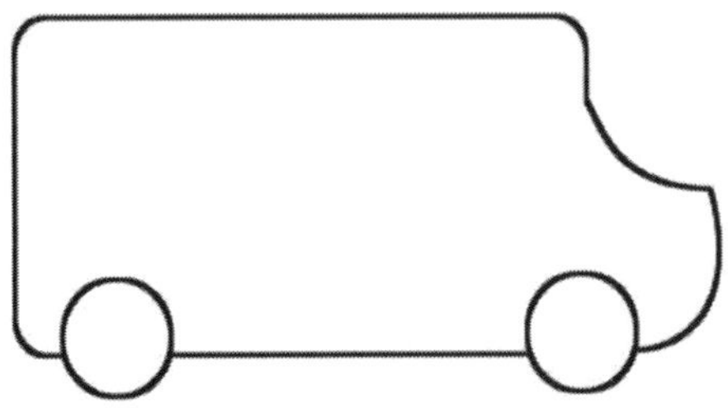

Show the number using ten frames

Find the number 4

1 3 2 6
1 4 5 7
6 8 6 5
8 9 7 4
2 9 0 3

Circle the Number

Name: ____________________ **Date:**__________

Circle the number that matches the amount of objects.

3 1 2 4	4 3 1 2	3 1 2 4
5 4 3 6	1 4 3 5	8 3 5 4
1 8 6 5	9 1 5 2	7 6 3 5

Name: ____________ Date: ____________

•Color it

4

•Find the numbers 4

1	2	5	2	8
3	4	4	10	1
4	3	1	5	5

•Trace and write it

4

Four

•Follow the numbers 4 through the maze

Start		4	4	4	4	6	5
3	1	2	2	2	4	4	5
3	3	3	3	3	3	Finish	

Name:

Date:

Read It!

Four

Write It!

Color It!

Four

Color It!

How many syllables?

3	4	5

Trace It!

Four

Find It!

Four	Two
One	Three

Write the missing number!

3 ☐ 5

Color 4 star!

☆ ☆ ☆ ☆ ☆
☆ ☆ ☆ ☆ ☆

Name: ____________ Date: ____________

I can read it!

Four

I can write it!

Four Four Four Four

I can color it!

Four

Find it!

One	Four
Two	Three

Circle it!

1	2	3	3
3	4	6	9
4	5	2	7

Name: ______________ Date: ______________

Count the numbers using the number line!

4 + 1 = ☐

0 1 2 3 4 5 6 7 8 9 10

4 + 2 = ☐

0 1 2 3 4 5 6 7 8 9 10

4 + 3 = ☐

0 1 2 3 4 5 6 7 8 9 10

Name: ______________ Date: ______________

1.Dab the Number 4

1 3 4 4 3

2.Color 4 star

3.Trace the number

4 4 4 4 4 4 4 4

4. Trace the number word

Four Four Four

Name:

Date:

Color 4 apples

Trace the number 4

Trace it

Circle the Number

Name: ______________________ Date:___________

Circle the number that matches the amount of objects.

5 4 3 6	7 3 4 5	3 1 2 4
5 4 3 6	1 8 7 5	8 7 5 4
9 8 6 5	4 1 3 2	7 9 8 6

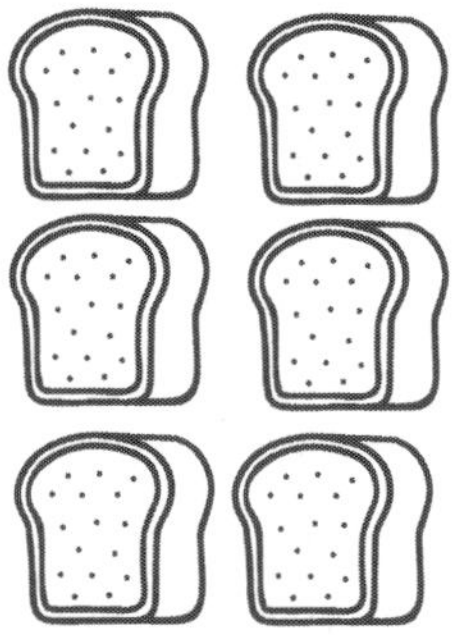

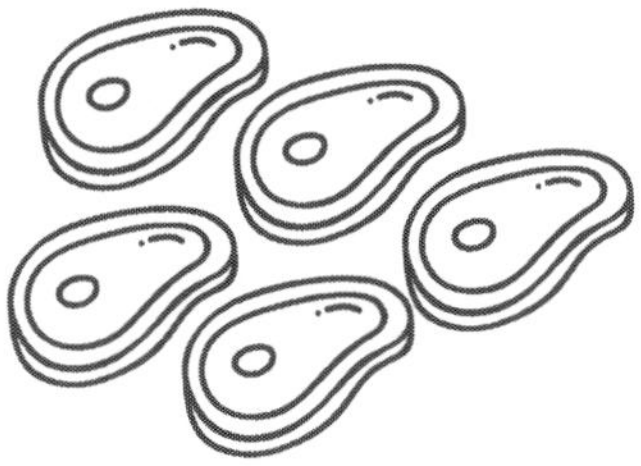

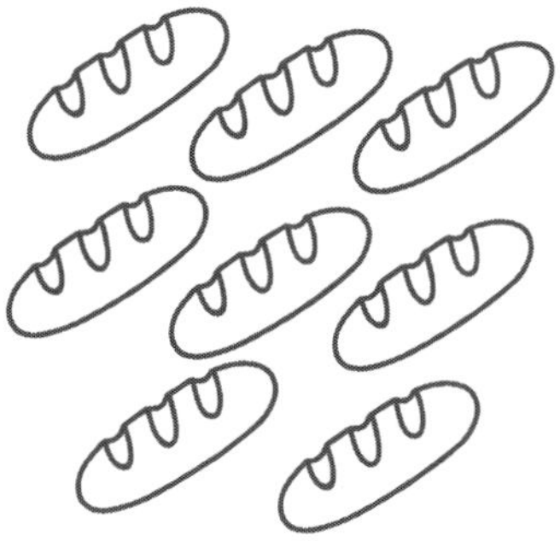

Name: Date:

5 Five

I can decompose one numbers:

5 6 7

5 5 5

I can Subtract using a number line

0 1 2 3 4 5 6 7 8 9 10

5 - 1 = ☐ 5 - 3 = ☐

5 - 2 = ☐ 5 - 2 = ☐

I can skip count by 5s

Name: ____________ Date: ____________

I Know My Numbers 5

Trace it

Five Five Five Five Five

5 5 5 5 5 5 5 5 5

Write the missing number

3 4 ☐

Color the number word

Five

Color 5 cloud

Draw 5 dot in the bus

Show the number using ten frames

Find the number 5

1 3 2 6
1 4 5 7
6 8 6 5
8 9 7 4
2 9 0 3

Circle the Number

Name: ____________________ Date:__________

Circle the number that matches the amount of objects.

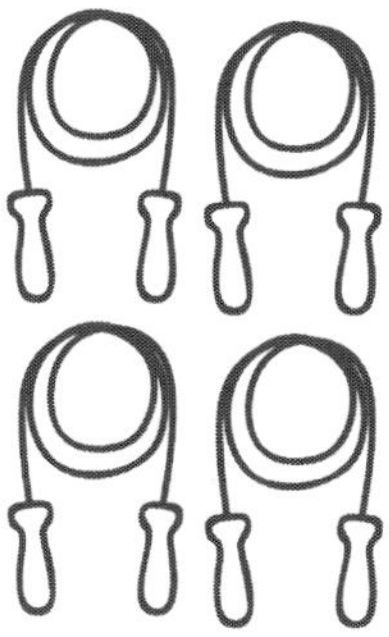

5 4 3 6	7 3 4 5	3 1 2 4
5 4 3 6	1 8 7 5	8 7 5 4
9 8 6 5	4 1 3 2	7 9 8 6

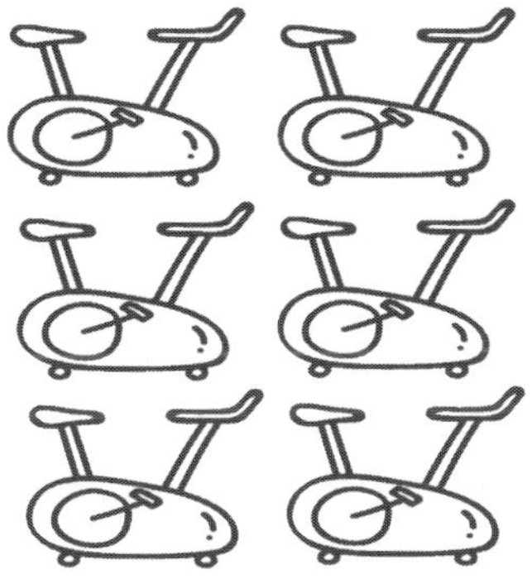

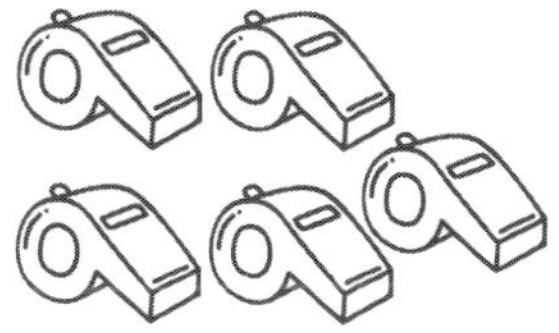

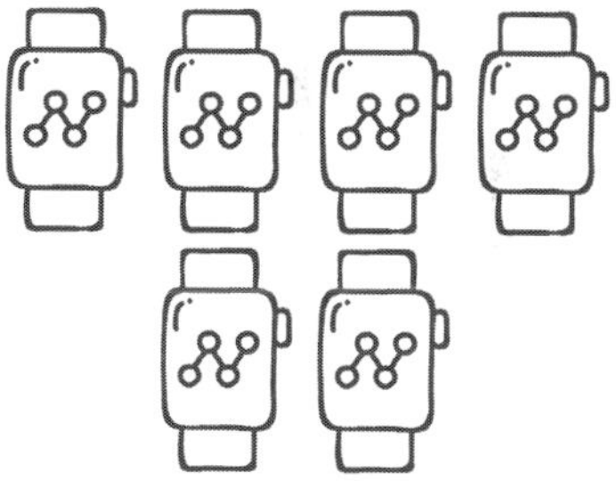

Name: ______________ Date: ______________

·Color it

5

·Find the numbers 5

1	2	5	2	8
3	4	4	10	1
4	3	1	5	5

·Trace and write it

5

Five

·Follow the numbers 5 through the maze

Start		5	5	5	5	5	5
3	1	2	2	2	4	4	5
3	3	3	3	3	3	Finish	

Name: ______________ Date: ______________

Read It!	Write It!
Five	

Color It!	Color It!
Five	How many syllables? 3 4 5

Trace It!	Find It!
Five	Four, Two, Five, Three

Write the missing number!	Color 5 star!
3 4 ☐	☆☆☆☆☆ ☆☆☆☆☆

Name:

Date:

I can read it!

Five

I can write it!

Five Five Five Five

I can color it!

Five

Find it!

Five	Four
Two	Three

Circle it!

1	2	3	3
3	4	6	5
4	5	2	7

Name: ______________________ Date: ______________________

Count the numbers using the number line!

4 + 4 = ☐

0 1 2 3 4 5 6 7 8 9 10

4 + 5 = ☐

0 1 2 3 4 5 6 7 8 9 10

5 + 1 = ☐

0 1 2 3 4 5 6 7 8 9 10

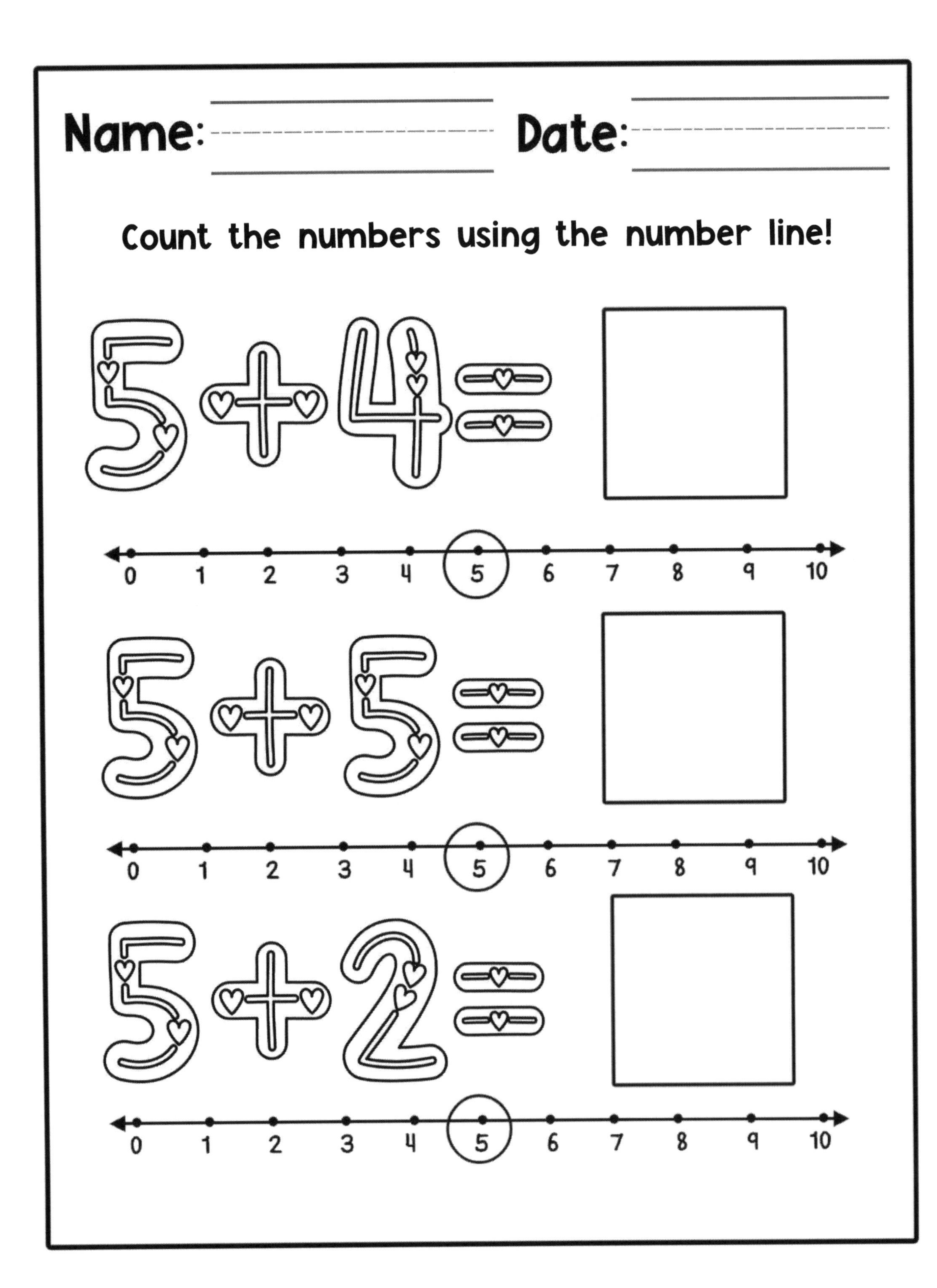
Name:
Date:
Count the numbers using the number line!
5+4=
0 1 2 3 4 5 6 7 8 9 10
5+5=
0 1 2 3 4 5 6 7 8 9 10
5+2=
0 1 2 3 4 5 6 7 8 9 10

Name:

Date:

1.Dab the Number 5

5 3 4 4 5

2.Color 5 star

3.Trace the number

5 5 5 5 5 5 5 5

4. Trace the number word

Five Five Five

Name:

Date:

Color 5 apples

Trace the number 5

5

Trace it

5 5 5 5 5 5 5

Five Five Five Five

Circle the Number

Name: ____________________ **Date:**__________

Circle the number that matches the amount of objects.

 5 4 3 6	 7 3 4 5	 3 1 2 4
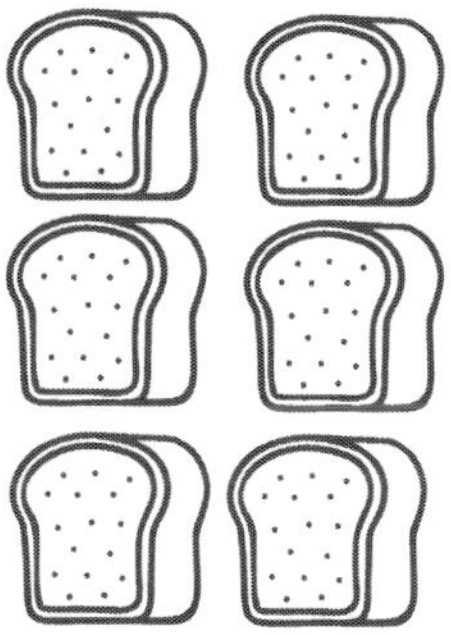 5 4 3 6	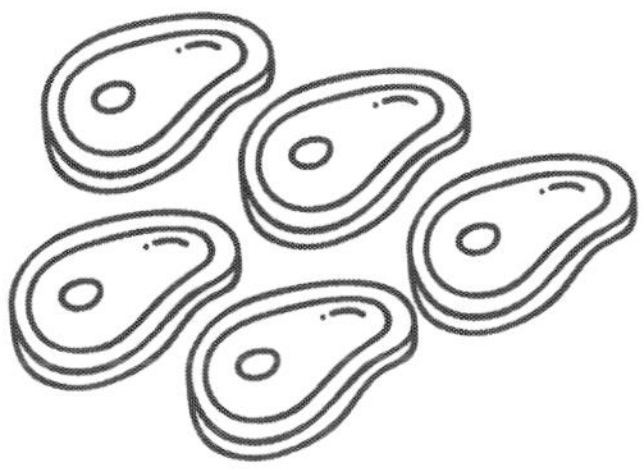 1 8 7 5	 8 7 5 4
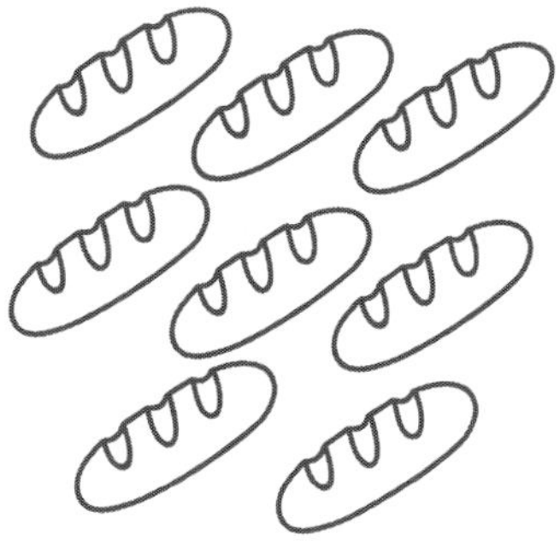 9 8 6 5	 4 1 3 2	 7 9 8 6

Name: Date:

6 Six

I can decompose one numbers:

6 7 8

6 6 6

I can Subtract using a number line

0 1 2 3 4 5 6 7 8 9 10

6 - 2 = ☐ 6 - 3 = ☐

6 - 3 = ☐ 6 - 2 = ☐

I can skip count by 6s

Name:

Date:

I Know My Numbers 6

Trace it

Six Six Six Six Six Six

6 6 6 6 6 6 6 6 6

Write the missing number

7 8

Color the number word

Six

Color 6 cloud

Draw 6 dot in the bus

Show the number using ten frames

Find the number 6

1 3 2 6
1 4 5 7
6 8 6 5
8 9 7 4
2 9 0 3

Circle the Number

Name: ____________________ Date:__________

Circle the number that matches the amount of objects.

 5 4 3 6	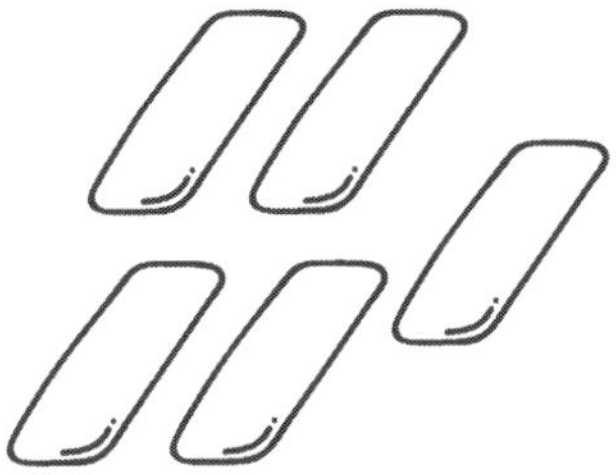 7 5 2 1	 5 1 2 4
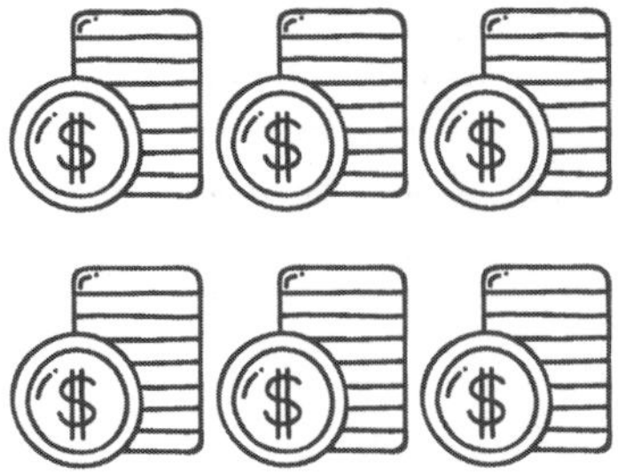 5 4 3 6	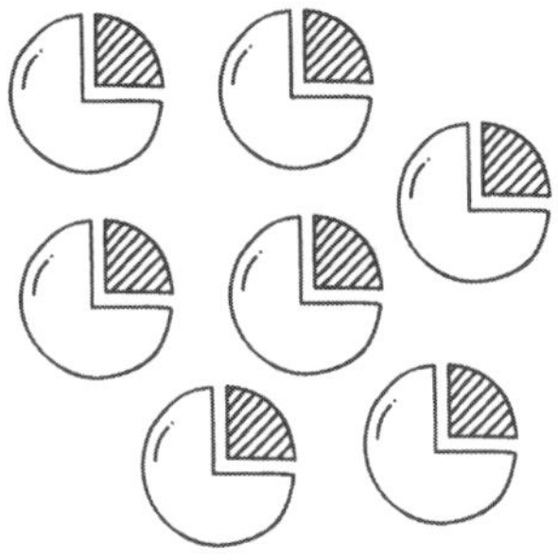 1 8 7 5	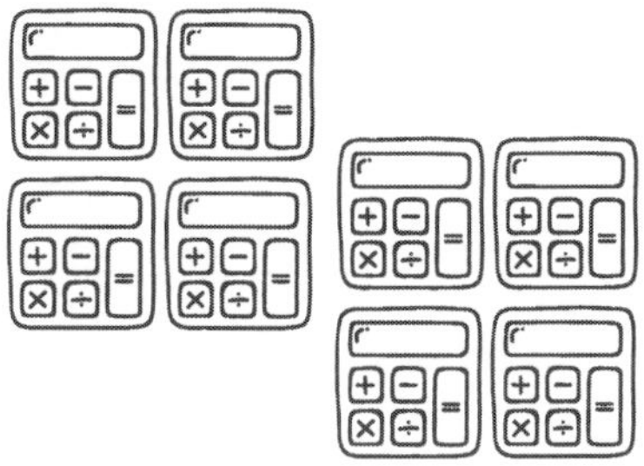 8 3 5 4
 1 9 2 5	 4 1 3 2	 3 4 1 2

Name: ____________ Date: ____________

•Color it

6

•Find the numbers 6

1	2	5	6	8
6	4	4	10	1
4	3	6	5	5

•Trace and write it

6

Six

•Follow the numbers 6 through the maze

Start		6	5	5	5	5	5
3	1	6	2	2	4	4	5
3	3	6	6	6	6	Finish	

Name:

Date:

Read It!

Six

Write It!

Color It!

Six

Color It!

How many syllables?

3	4	5

Trace It!

Six

Find It!

Four	Six
Five	Three

Write the missing number!

☐ 7 8

Color 6 star!

☆ ☆ ☆ ☆ ☆
☆ ☆ ☆ ☆ ☆

Name:

Date:

I can read it!

Six

I can write it!

Six Six Six Six Six

I can color it!

Six

Find it!

Five	Six
Two	Three

Circle it!

1	2	3	3
3	4	6	5
6	5	2	7

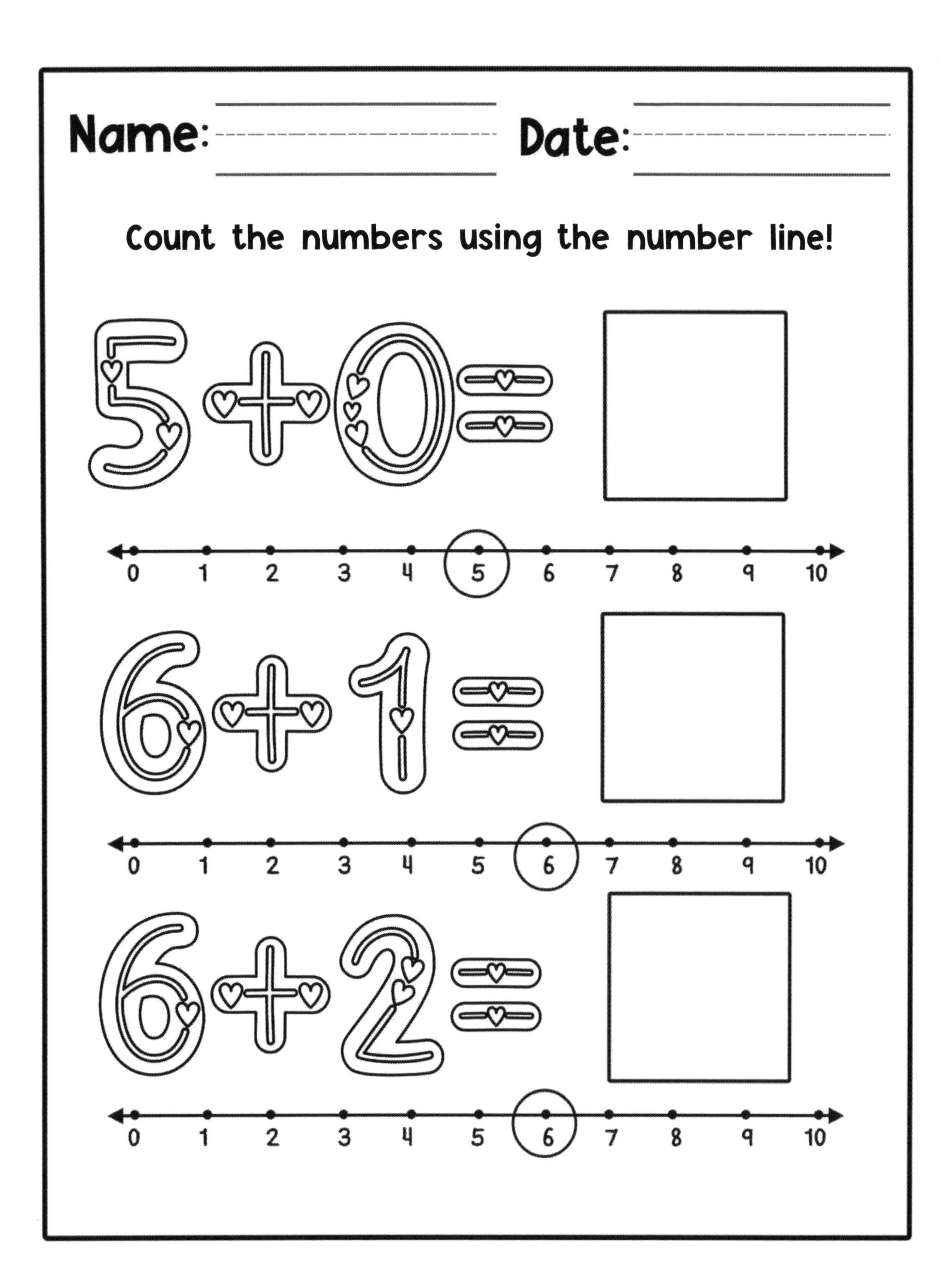
Name:
Date:
Count the numbers using the number line!
5+0=
0 1 2 3 4 5 6 7 8 9 10
6+1=
0 1 2 3 4 5 6 7 8 9 10
6+2=
0 1 2 3 4 5 6 7 8 9 10

Name: ____________ Date: ____________

1.Dab the Number 6

5 6 4 6 5

2.Color 6 star

3.Trace the number

6 6 6 6 6 6 6

4. Trace the number word

Six Six Six

Name:

Date:

Color 6 apples

Trace the number 6

6

Trace it

6 6 6 6 6 6 6

Six Six Six Six Six

Circle the Number

Name: ____________________ Date:__________

Circle the number that matches the amount of objects.

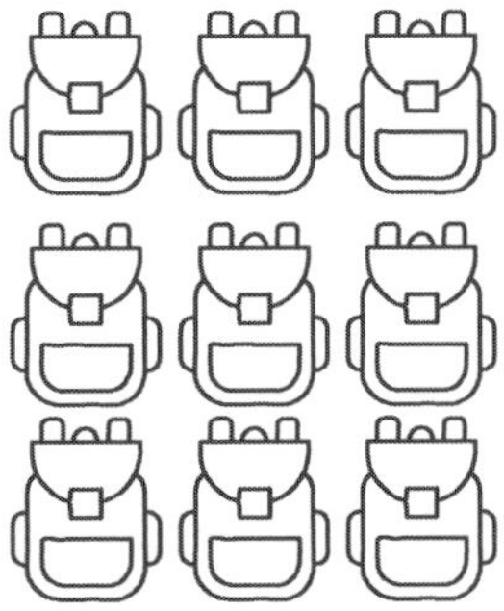 7 8 9 6	 4 5 7 6	 3 1 2 6
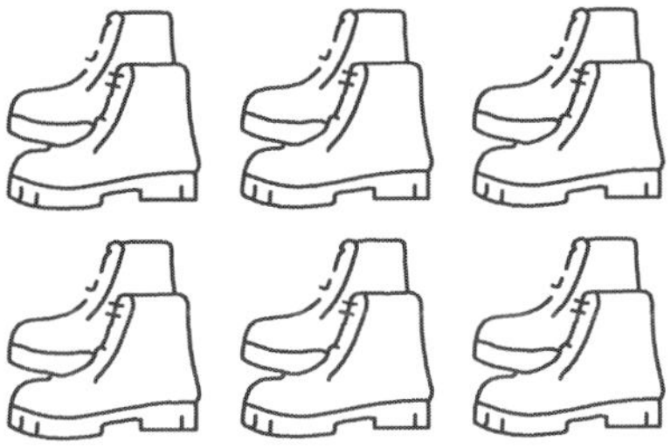 5 4 3 6	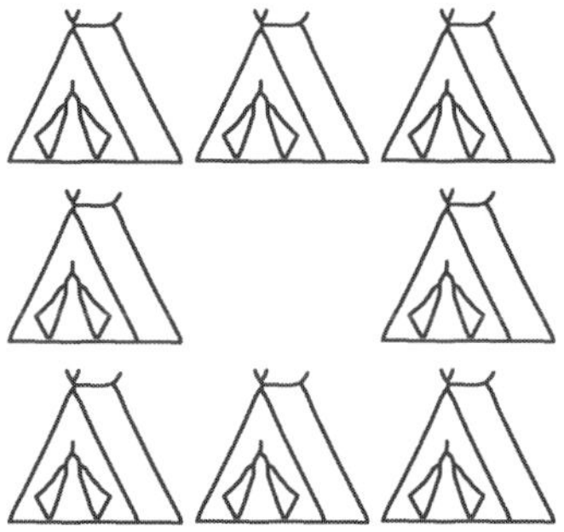 1 8 7 5	 1 2 3 4
 4 3 7 5	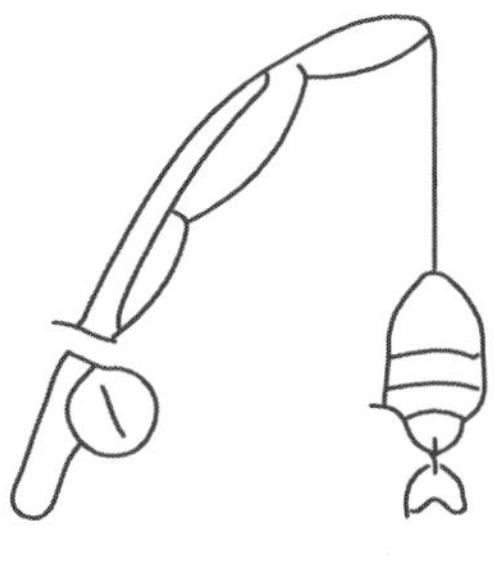 0 1 3 2	 7 6 3 5

Name:

Date:

7 Seven

I can decompose one numbers:

10

7

8

7

9

7

I can Subtract using a number line

0 1 2 3 4 5 6 7 8 9 10

7 - 2 =

7 - 3 =

7 - 3 =

7 - 2 =

I can skip count by 7s

Name: ______________ Date: ______________

I Know My Numbers 7

Trace it

Seven Seven Seven

7 7 7 7 7 7 7 7 7

Write the missing number

6 ☐ 8

Color the number word

Seven

Color 7 cloud

Draw 7 dot in the bus

Show the number using ten frames

Find the number 7

1 3 2 6

1 4 5 7

6 8 6 5

8 9 7 4

2 9 0 3

Circle the Number

Name: ____________________ **Date:**__________

Circle the number that matches the amount of objects.

5 4 3 6	7 9 8 6	3 1 2 4
5 4 3 6	1 8 7 5	8 3 5 4
1 3 2 5	4 1 3 2	7 6 3 5

Name: ____________ Date: ____________

•Color it

7

•Find the numbers 7

7	2	5	6	8
6	4	4	10	7
7	3	6	5	5

•Trace and write it

7

Seven

•Follow the numbers 7 through the maze

<table>
<tr><td colspan="2">Start</td><td>6</td><td>5</td><td>5</td><td>5</td><td>5</td><td>5</td></tr>
<tr><td>3</td><td>7</td><td>7</td><td>7</td><td>7</td><td>7</td><td>4</td><td>5</td></tr>
<tr><td>3</td><td>3</td><td>6</td><td>6</td><td>6</td><td>7</td><td colspan="2">Finish</td></tr>
</table>

Name: ______________________ Date: ______________________

Read It!	Write It!
Seven	______________________

Color It!	Color It!
Seven	How many syllables? 3 4 5

Trace It!	Find It!
Seven	Seven Six Five Three

Write the missing number!	Color 7 star!
6 ☐ 8	☆☆☆☆☆ ☆☆☆☆☆

Name: ____________ Date: ____________

I can read it!

Seven

I can write it!

Seven Seven Seven

I can color it!

Seven

Find it!

Five	Six
Seven	Three

Circle it!

1	7	3	3
3	4	6	5
6	5	2	7

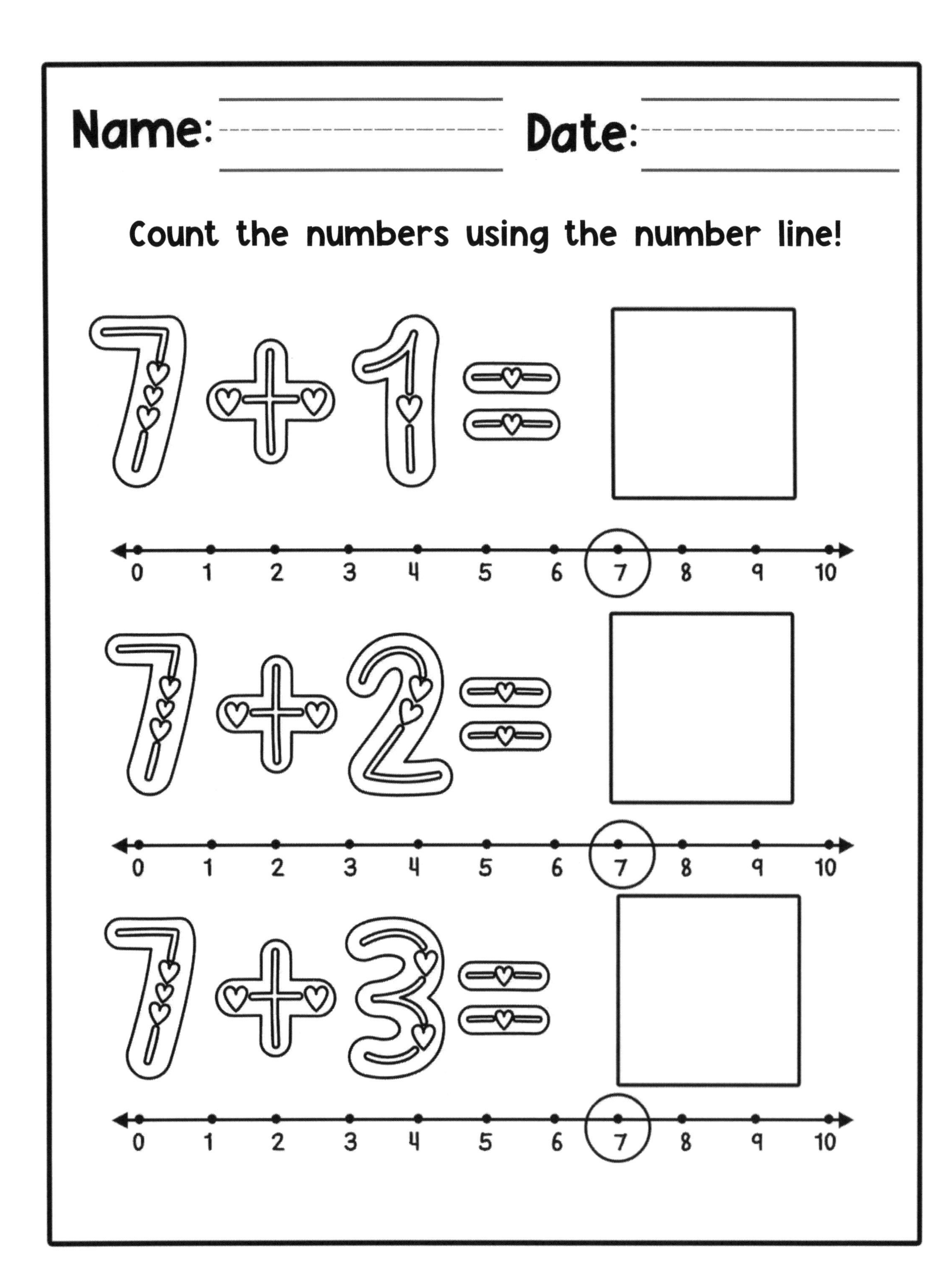
Name:
Date:
Count the numbers using the number line!
7 + 1 =
0 1 2 3 4 5 6 7 8 9 10
7 + 2 =
0 1 2 3 4 5 6 7 8 9 10
7 + 3 =
0 1 2 3 4 5 6 7 8 9 10

Name: ____________ Date: ____________

1.Dab the Number 7

5 6 7 6 7

2.Color 7 star

3.Trace the number

7 7 7 7 7 7 7

4. Trace the number word

Seven Seven

Name:

Date:

Color 7 apples

Trace the number 7

7

Trace it

7 7 7 7 7 7 7

Seven Seven Seven

Circle the Number

Name: ____________________ Date:__________

Circle the number that matches the amount of objects.

 5 4 3 6	 7 9 8 6	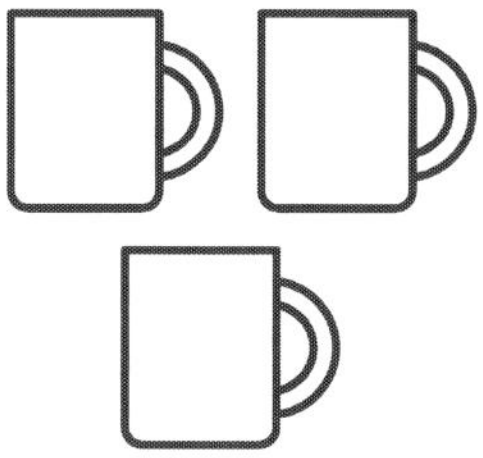 3 1 2 4
 5 4 3 6	 1 8 7 5	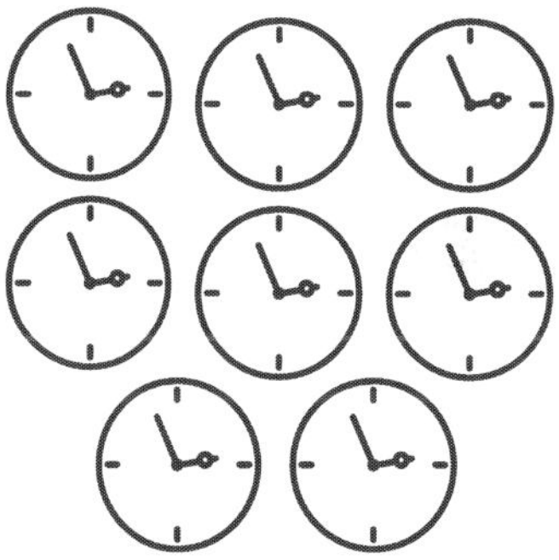 8 3 5 4
 1 3 2 5	 4 1 3 2	 7 6 3 5

Name: ______________ Date: ______________

8 Eight

I can decompose one numbers:

10	8	9
8	8	8

I can Subtract using a number line

0 1 2 3 4 5 6 7 8 9 10

8 - 6 = ☐   8 - 1 = ☐

8 - 5 = ☐   8 - 2 = ☐

I can skip count by 8s

◯ ◯ ◯ ◯

Name: ______________________ Date: ______________________

I Know My Numbers 8

Trace it

Eight Eight Eight Eight

8 8 8 8 8 8 8 8 8 8

Write the missing number

6 7 ☐

Color the number word

Eight

Color 8 cloud

Draw 8 dot in the bus

Show the number using ten frames

Find the number 8

1	3	2	6
1	4	5	7
6	8	6	5
8	9	7	4
2	9	0	3

Circle the Number

Name: ____________________ **Date:** __________

Circle the number that matches the amount of objects.

 3 1 2 4	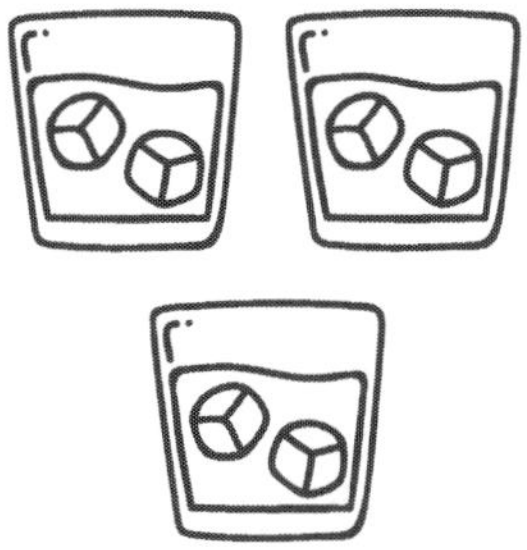 4 3 1 2	 3 1 2 4
 5 4 3 6	 1 4 3 5	 8 3 5 4
 1 8 6 5	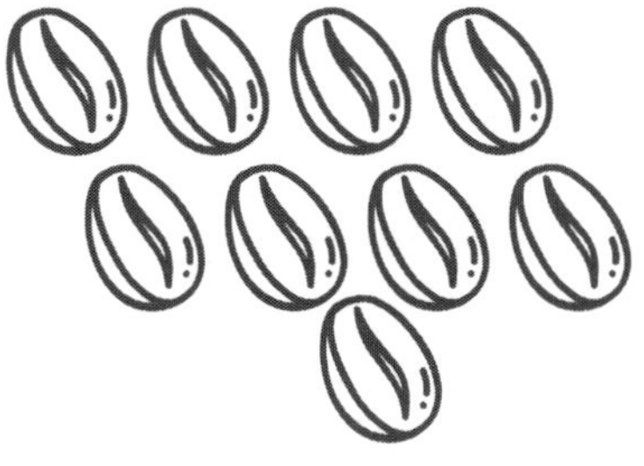 9 1 5 2	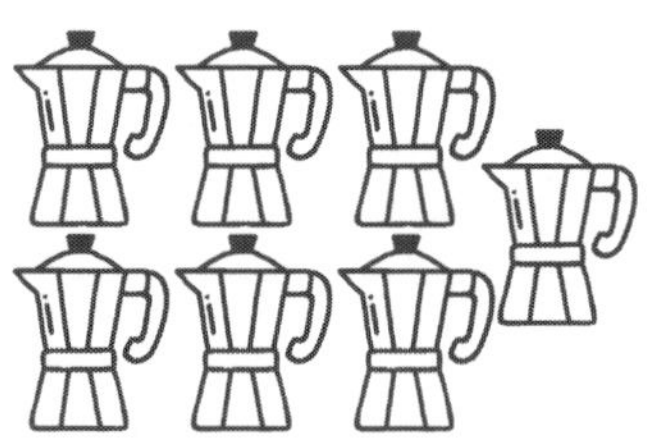 7 6 3 5

Name: ____________ Date: ____________

•Color it

8

•Find the numbers 8

7	2	5	6	8
8	4	4	10	7
7	8	6	5	5

•Trace and write it

8

Eight

•Follow the numbers 8 through the maze

Start		8	8	5	5	5	5
3	7	7	8	8	7	4	5
3	3	6	6	8	8	Finish	

Name:

Date:

Read It!

Eight

Write It!

Color It!

Eight

Color It!

How many syllables?

5	4	6

Trace It!

Eight

Find It!

Seven	Six
Eight	Three

Write the missing number!

6 7 ☐

Color 8 star!

☆ ☆ ☆ ☆ ☆
☆ ☆ ☆ ☆ ☆

Name:

Date:

I can read it!

Eight

I can write it!

Seven Seven Seven

I can color it!

Eight

Find it!

Five	Six
Seven	Eight

Circle it!

1	7	3	3
3	4	6	5
6	8	2	8

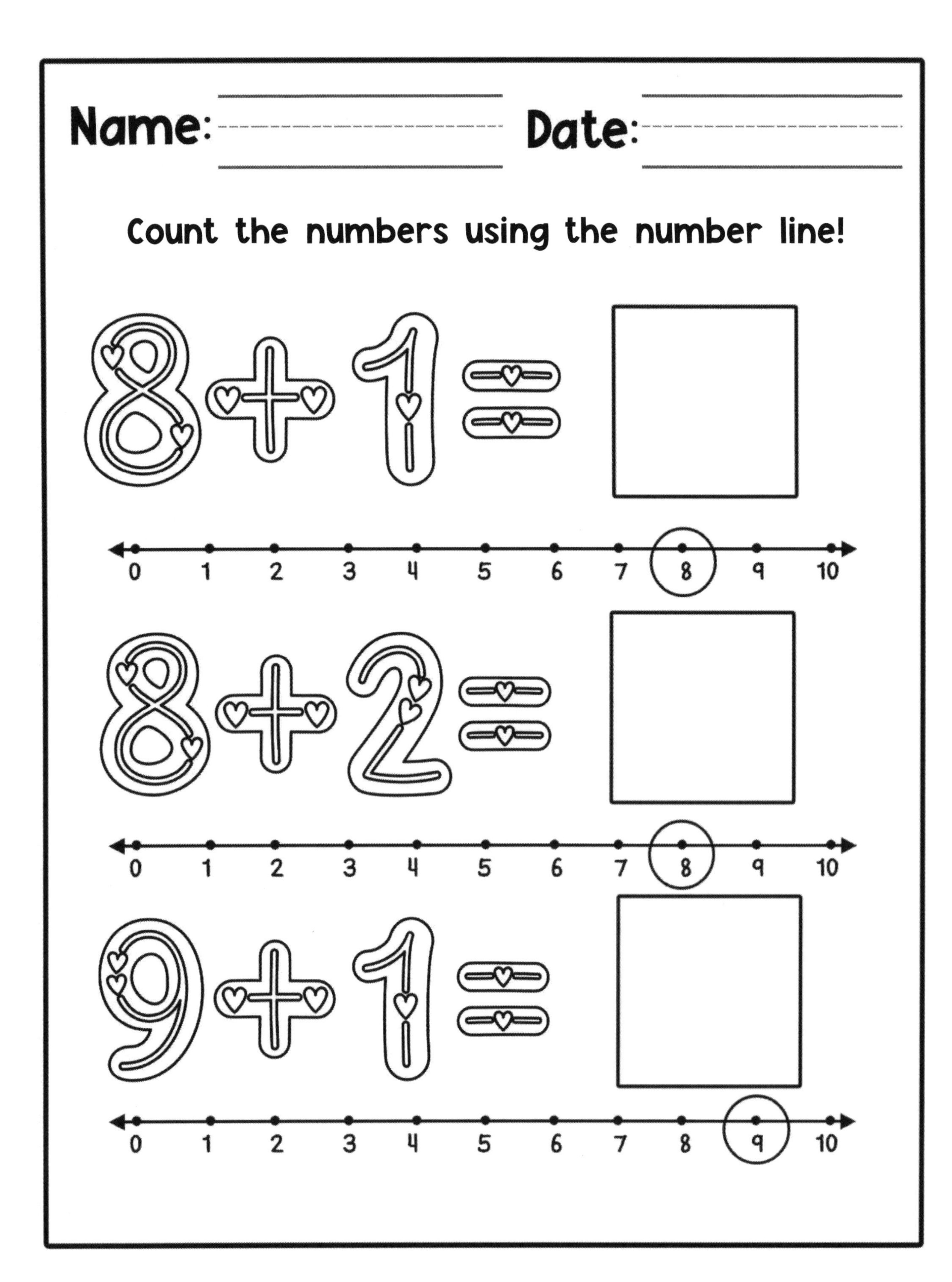
Name:
Date:
Count the numbers using the number line!
8+1=
0 1 2 3 4 5 6 7 8 9 10
8+2=
0 1 2 3 4 5 6 7 8 9 10
9+1=
0 1 2 3 4 5 6 7 8 9 10

Name: ______________ Date: ______________

1.Dab the Number 8

8 8 7 6 7

2.Color 8 star

3.Trace the number

8 8 8 8 8 8 8 8

4. Trace the number word

Eight Eight

Name: ________________ Date: ________________

Color 8 apples

Trace the number 8

8

Trace it

8 8 8 8 8 8 8

Eight Eight Eight

Name: Date:

9 Nine

I can decompose one numbers:

10 11 9

9 9 9

I can Subtract using a number line

0 1 2 3 4 5 6 7 8 9 10

9 - 6 = 9 - 4 =

9 - 5 = 9 - 2 =

I can skip count by 9s

Circle the Number

Name: ______________________ Date:___________

Circle the number that matches the amount of objects.

 3 1 2 4	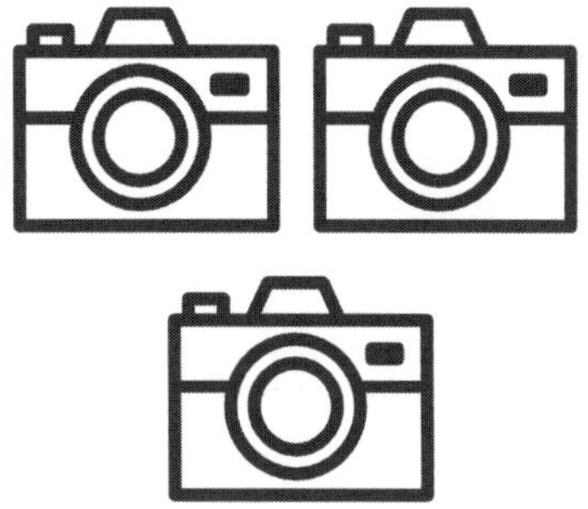 4 3 1 2	 3 1 2 4
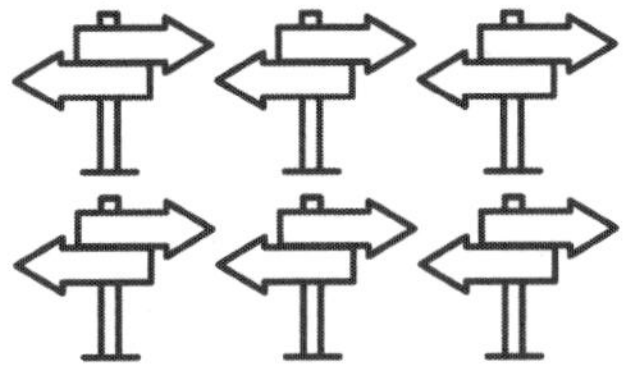 5 4 3 6	 1 4 3 5	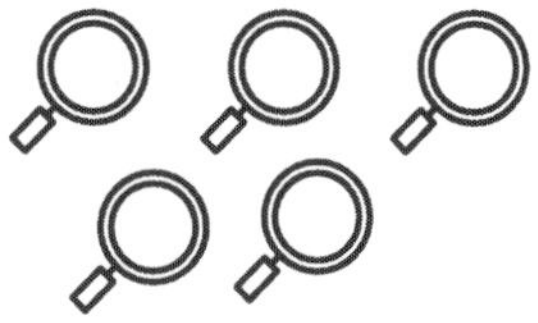 8 3 5 4
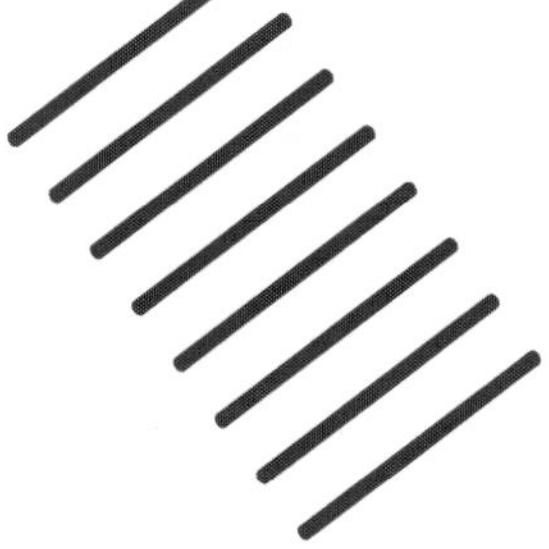 1 8 6 5	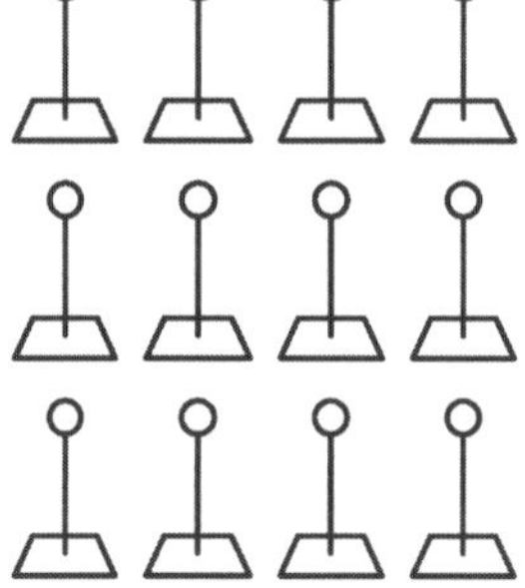 9 1 5 2	 7 6 3 5

Name: ____________ Date: ____________

I Know My Numbers 9

Trace it

Nine Nine Nine Nine

9 9 9 9 9 9 9 9 9 9

Write the missing number

8 ☐ 10

Color the number word

Nine

Color 9 cloud

Draw 9 dot in the bus

Show the number using ten frames

Find the number 9

1 3 2 6
1 4 5 7
6 8 6 5
8 9 7 4
2 9 0 3

Circle the Number

Name: ____________________ Date:__________

Circle the number that matches the amount of objects.

 5 4 3 6	 7 3 4 5	 3 1 2 4
 Milk Milk Milk Milk Milk Milk 5 4 3 6	 1 8 7 5	 8 7 5 4
 9 8 6 5	 4 1 3 2	 7 9 8 6

Name: ______________ Date: ______________

•Color it

9

•Find the numbers 9

7	9	5	6	8
8	4	9	10	7
7	8	6	9	5

•Trace and write it

9

Nine

•Follow the numbers 9 through the maze

Start		8	9	9	9	9	5
9	9	9	9	8	7	9	5
3	3	6	6	8	8	Finish	

Name:

Date:

Read It!

Nine

Write It!

Color It!

Nine

Color It!

How many syllables?

5	4	6

Trace It!

Nine

Find It!

Seven	Six
Eight	Nine

Write the missing number!

8 ☐ 10

Color 9 star!

Name: ____________________ Date: ____________________

I can read it!

Nine

I can write it!

Nine Nine Nine Nine

I can color it!

Nine

Find it!

Five	Nine
Seven	Eight

Circle it!

9	7	3	3
3	4	6	5
6	8	9	8

Name: ____________ Date: ____________

1.Dab the Number 9

8 8 9 9 7

2.Color 9 star

3.Trace the number

9 9 9 9 9 9 9 9

4. Trace the number word

Nine Nine Nine

Name: ____________ Date: ____________

Color 9 apples

Trace the number 9

9

Trace it

9 9 9 9 9 9 9

Nine Nine Nine

Name: ______________ Date: ______________

10 Ten

I can decompose one numbers:

10 11 12

10 10 10

I can Subtract using a number line

0 1 2 3 4 5 6 7 8 9 10

10 - 6 = ☐ 10 - 4 = ☐

10 - 5 = ☐ 10 - 5 = ☐

I can skip count by 10s

○ ○ ○ ○

Name: ____________ Date: ____________

I Know My Numbers 10

Trace it

Ten Ten Ten Ten Ten

10 10 10 10 10 10 10 10

Write the missing number

8 9 ☐

Color the number word

Ten

Color 10 cloud

Draw 10 dot in the bus

Show the number using ten frames

Find the number 10

1	3	2	6
1	10	10	1
6	8	6	5
8	9	7	4
2	9	0	3

Circle the Number

Name: ______________________ Date:___________

Circle the number that matches the amount of objects.

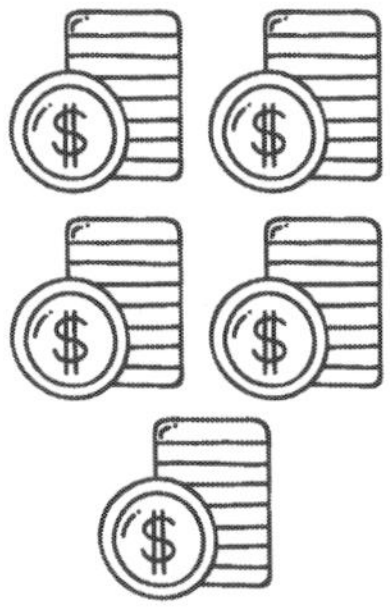 5 4 3 6	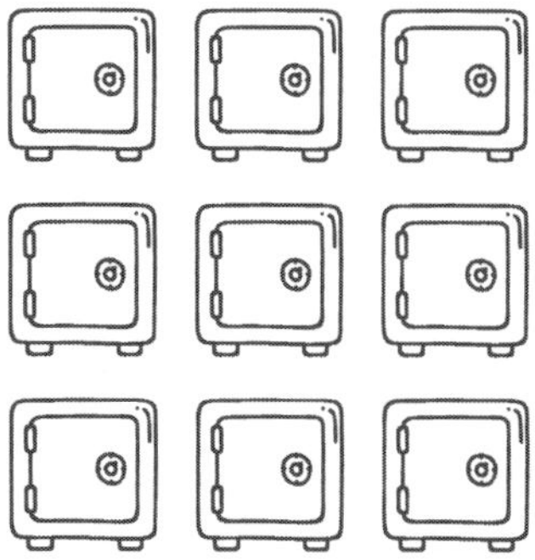 7 9 8 6	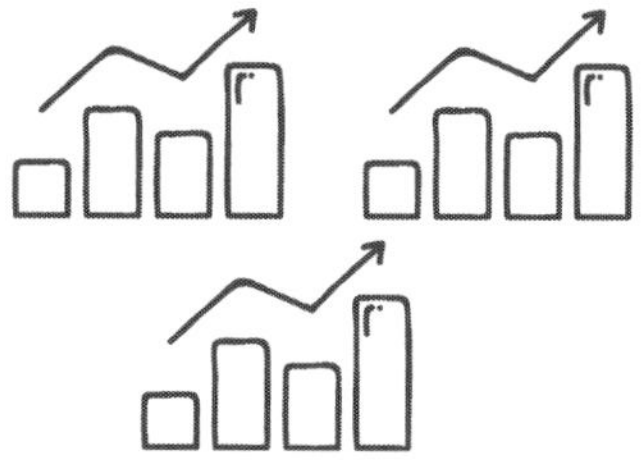 3 1 2 4
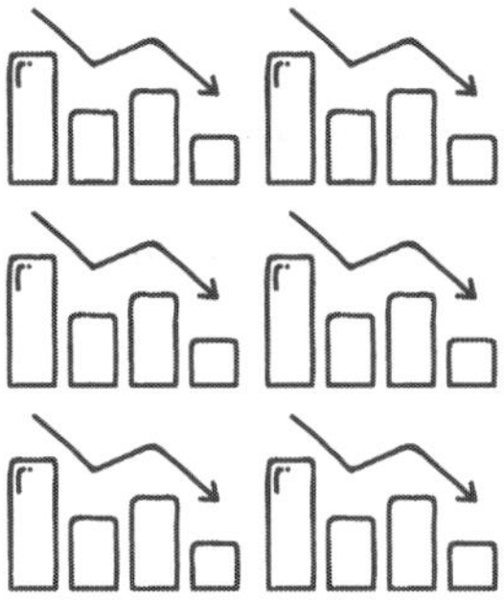 5 4 3 6	 1 8 7 5	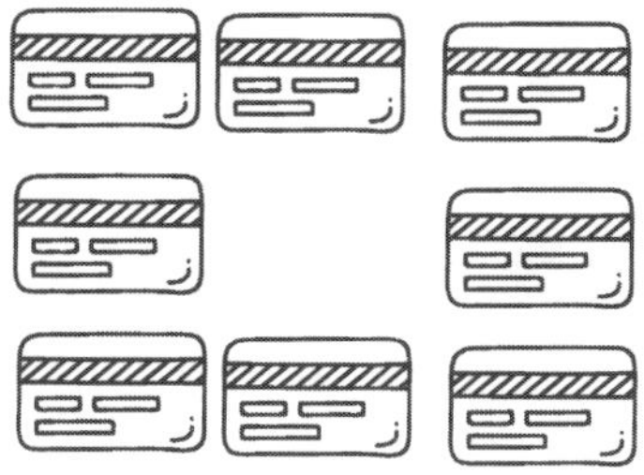 8 3 5 4
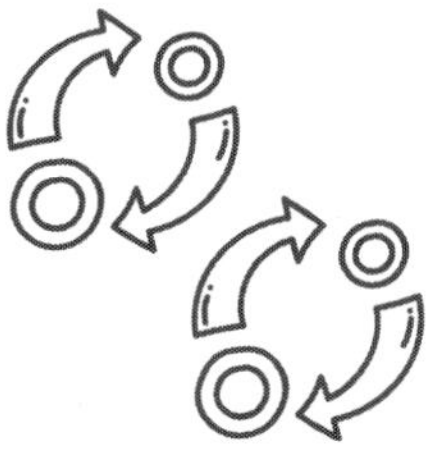 1 3 2 5	 4 1 3 2	 7 6 3 5

Name: ______________ Date: ______________

·Color it

10

·Find the numbers 10

7	9	10	10	8
8	10	9	10	7
7	8	6	9	5

·Trace and write it

10

Ten

·Follow the numbers 10 through the maze

Start		10	10	10	10	9	5
9	9	9	9	8	10	9	5
3	3	6	6	8	10	Finish	

Name: ______________ Date: ______________

Read It!	Write It!
Ten	

Color It!	Color It!
Ten	How many syllables? 5 3 6

Trace It!	Find It!
Ten	Ten Six Eight Nine

Write the missing number!	Color 10 star!
8 9 ☐	☆☆☆☆☆ ☆☆☆☆☆

Name: ____________ Date: ____________

I can read it!

Ten

I can write it!

Ten Ten Ten Ten

I can color it!

Ten

Find it!

Five	Nine
Ten	Eight

Circle it!

9	10	3	3
3	4	6	5
6	8	10	8

Name: ____________ Date: ____________

1.Dab the Number 10

10 8 9 9 10

2.Color 10 star

3.Trace the number

10 10 10 10 10 10

4. Trace the number word

Ten Ten Ten

Name: ____________ Date: ____________

Color 10 apples

Trace the number 10

10

Trace it

10 10 10 10 10

Ten Ten Ten Ten

Circle the Number

Name: ____________________ Date:__________

Circle the number that matches the amount of objects.

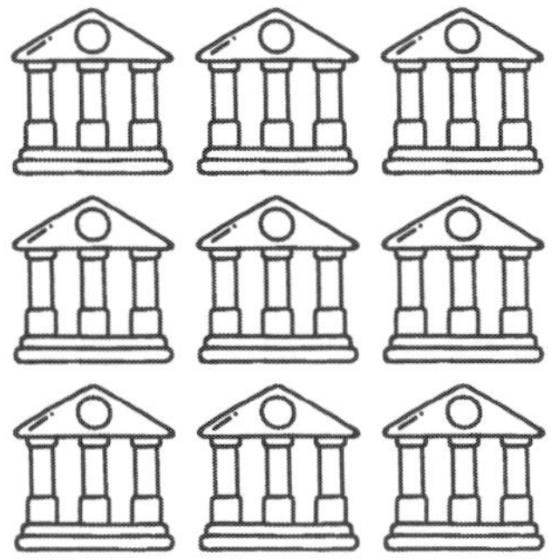 7 8 9 6	 4 5 7 6	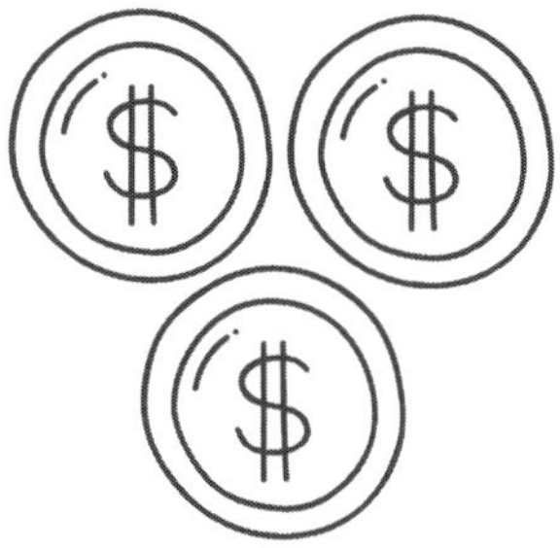 3 1 2 6
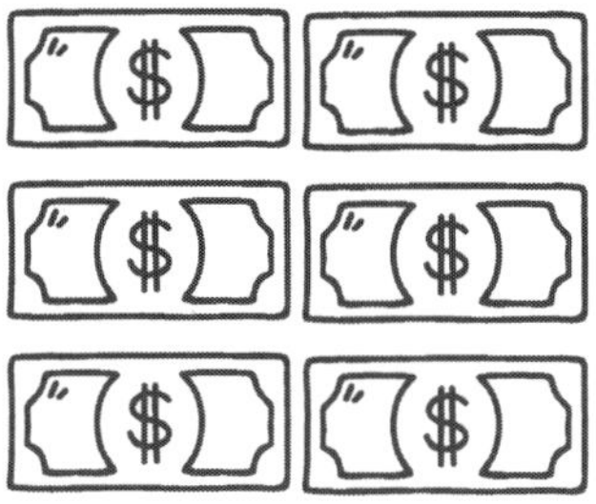 5 4 3 6	 1 8 7 5	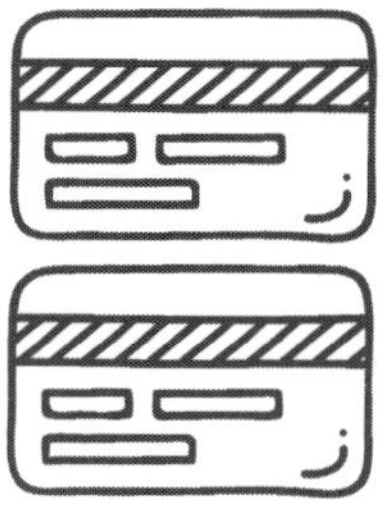 1 2 3 4
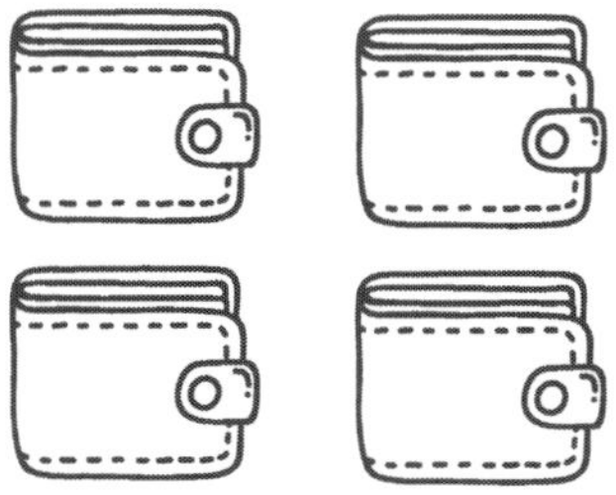 4 3 7 5	 0 1 3 2	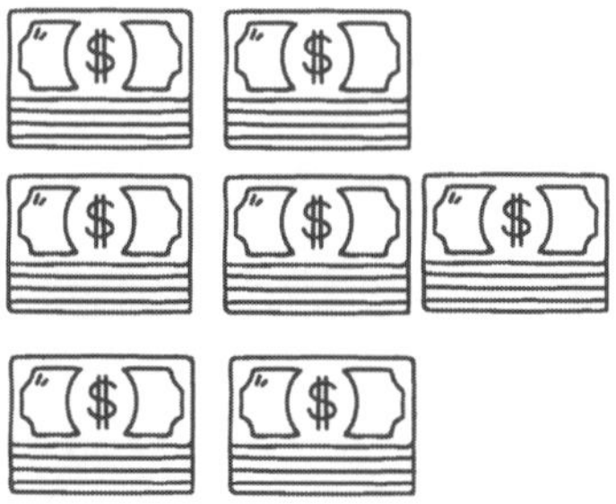 7 6 3 5

Made in the USA
Middletown, DE
22 August 2022